ACTS OF
DEFIANCE

ACTS OF DEFIANCE

How
Self-giving
Love Inspires
Acts of Grace,
Forgiveness,
and Compassion

ANTHONY
M. COTTRELL

XULON PRESS

Xulon Press
2301 Lucien Way #415
Maitland, FL 32751
407.339.4217
www.xulonpress.com

Paperback ISBN-13: 978-1-6628-5340-1
Ebook ISBN-13: 978-1-6628-5341-8

To mom and dad—Bridget and Mark Cottrell.

Table of Contents

INTRODUCTION

Acts that Defy

I grew up in the church. I accepted Jesus into my heart when I was four or five. At least, that is what I have been told by my mom. Sometimes I question the validity of such a testimony. I mean, can a four or five year old really understand the decision they are making? I don't know. What I do know is that I grew up loving Jesus and loving the church. I also know that God later confronted me with a decision moment when I was in middle school that radically shaped my story.

I also went to a Christian school from 1st grade through 12th grade. I had Bible class every single day. I knew what I believed. That is, until I didn't. Later in life I had a number of experiences that did not fit very nicely into the doctrinal boxes I had neatly organized on the intellectual shelves of my mind. Part of what became so perplexing to me was that it seemed like a lot of people I knew—from my church, my Christian school, and from other little Christian environments—were going to heaven, but were indistinguishable from other nice, moral American families. I began to question what exactly it means to be a Christian.

Unfortunately, my Christian experience had exposed me to "Christians" who believed all the right things, but were mean, bitter, and judgmental. Sadly, I have known professing unbelievers who were more sincere and kind than some Christians. Maybe you have too. Now, I do not believe I hold the gavel when it comes to people's eternal destinies. I believe there are a lot of people who are going to heaven and are "Christians," but, for whatever reason, they are not living in light of the good news. They have accepted the gospel, but they have not allowed it to transform them.

I also know a fair number of well-intentioned believers who are really concerned about doctrinal correctness. Doctrine is important. I care a lot about theology and doctrine. But, Jesus summed up the point of the Law and doctrine when he called us to love God and love people.[1] Paul goes so far as to say that if we do not have love we gain *nothing*. Paul doesn't let us off the hook by simply allowing us to define love as merely not hating other people. He describes love in some pretty self-giving and sacrificial ways. Love is at the core patient, kind, forgiving, gracious, and persistently hopeful.[2] When our efforts to defend sound doctrine turn mean, they miss the point.

I have come to believe that being a Christian is not as much about what we believe doctrinally (as important as that is) as it is about actually following the way of Jesus. Often our gospel messages focus so much on the last week of Jesus' life that we tend to view the life and ministry of Jesus like the opening

---

[1] Matthew 22:36-40

[2] 1 Corinthians 13

trailers to a movie. Some people like to arrive to view them and others show up intentionally late just for the feature film. Jesus' life and ministry and teachings are inseparable from his death and resurrection. All that Jesus said and did was in complete harmony with the final act. It is a not a "take it or leave it" kind of message.

When we take following Jesus seriously and we allow our lives to be affected by the gospels, the things Jesus said and did will start to challenge our paradigms just like they did when he said or did them around his original audience. When we read that Jesus reached out and touched someone that was suffering from a repulsive skin disease, our aversion to getting involved in the messy parts of other people's lives gets confronted. Jesus' radical self-giving love and relentless compassion challenges our tendency to be self-focused. His teachings on forgiveness are almost offensive to our sense of justice. The grace he offers seems to have no boundaries. Each of these expressions of the Kingdom are significantly more challenging than simply mentally affirming a few correct doctrinal beliefs, and each of these realities defy our natural bent.

My own spiritual journey and my years serving in pastoral ministry have taught me that the thing God wants to do in our hearts is to form Christ in us. We are destined to be consumed by the self-giving love that God displayed on the cross in Jesus. The love and grace shown on the cross will call us to embody the same love and grace towards others. When we truly understand his forgiveness towards us, we will find that we *have to forgive*. Forgiving as Christ forgave is not optional because it is actually the appropriate response to his grace in our lives. It is part of authentically repenting and believing the gospel. As his love consumes us, his compassion will be birthed in our hearts.

Self-giving love, grace, forgiveness and compassion: I have found that God desires our hearts to be shaped by these powerful forces and there are some major shifts that have to happen in our lives for this to take place. The transformation will require the surrendering of some things. Death always precedes resurrection.

Acts of Defiance is about this transformation process. I titled the book *Acts of Defiance* because I have found that self-giving love threatens my tendency towards self-preservation, grace feels like a limited resource that I should give out sparingly, forgiveness is the hardest thing about the Christian life, and compassion often calls me to empathize with people I'd rather ignore. In other words, the way of Jesus stands in defiant contrast to the way of our sin broken hearts. Each of these Kingdom realities, especially once acted upon in tangible ways, is an act that defies the kingdom of darkness. Each act that is in alignment with the way of Jesus carries the power to change the world. But first, we must allow them to change us.

What To Expect

I have structured this book around this central idea: the love, grace, forgiveness and compassion of Jesus calls us to reflect self-giving love, grace, forgiveness, and compassion. In order for us to reflect Jesus more clearly and purely, our selfishness, legalism, desires for revenge, and judgmental attitudes have to be confronted, surrendered, and transformed.

We will first talk about how we need to be willing for our hearts and minds to be challenged. We do not grow when we preserve and protect our natural tendencies. We grow spiritually when we open our hearts up to the truth and conviction of the Holy Spirit.

The subsequent chapters will alternate between the natural bent of the heart and the way of Jesus. One chapter will focus on selfishness, the next will focus on self-giving love and so forth. The chapters that focus on our bent towards sin will be full of self-incriminating stories from my life. You see, I believe we are all sinners. As some have said, "the ground is level at the cross."[3] What I am sharing with you in these pages are parts of my journey. Some of those parts are still in process. Meaning, I have not arrived and I still act selfish and want revenge sometimes. I'm still prone to being judgmental. I am still engaging in ongoing acts of defiance as I seek to be shaped into the likeness of Jesus.

The final chapter will tie it all together by suggesting some ways that you can act upon these heart shifts. My hope is that, perhaps, the Holy Spirit will illuminate some things in your heart that you then surrender to him. In the process, I hope that you start participating in acts of defiance.

---

[3] I am not sure who said it first, but I have heard it from various sources.

CHAPTER 1

Mind Shift

J ust over six years ago I became a parent. Being a parent is
a unique joy and honor. I can't really describe it. Being a
parent has taught me a lot about God's love for us as his children. It has also taught me a lot about myself. I thought I was
somewhat Christ-like before having children. Now, I sometimes wonder if I am even saved.

Ok, not really, but I have found myself doing and feeling
and saying things that I am not proud of. Things that call into
question my sanctification. The other day our son was having
a tantrum. You know—the kind that makes you stare in dis-
belief, dumbfounded. He was screaming and would not stop.
I screamed as loud and as obnoxiously as I could straight in
his face. I am not proud of it, but sometimes you do what you
gotta do. He stopped screaming, so at that moment I counted
it as a shameful victory. Maybe you can relate.

What has become painfully obvious to me is the lack of
patience I have. Before having kids, I would have said that I
am a fairly patient, laid-back person. I wouldn't have described
myself as having a temper or anger issues. After kids... well,

that is a different story. Don't get me wrong. I love my kids so much that it is scary sometimes. I genuinely enjoy spending time with them. But, they're little sinful humans and sometimes their sinfulness collides with my sinfulness in ways that aren't so pretty.

Have you ever faced a new stage in life, an unexpected trial, or a new challenge that brought things to the surface you didn't know were there?

I'm a pastor in a denominational tradition that takes seriously the call to be holy. Our movement believes God's Spirit, the same one that raised Christ from the dead, is alive and at work in us, sanctifying us to look more and more like Jesus. Now, just in case those two words—holiness and sanctification—are a little "churchy," let me define them.

Holiness is an attribute of God that we are called to reflect. God's holiness describes his wholly otherness and his purity. God is wholly other in the sense that his divine nature is unlike anything else in creation. He is the uncreated one. God is also pure in every sense of the word. In the Scriptures, things that were holy were things that had been consecrated or "set apart for the purposes of God."

We, as image bearers, were created for the purposes of God. We are called to be holy. Sin infects our lives though. When we come to Christ, the Holy Spirit indwells our lives and sanctifies us. Sanctification is the process of God purifying those things that do not reflect his purity in love and action. I like to think of it like a refinement process.

The church I am a part of believes that the work of sanctification can radically transform our lives on this side of heaven. When Paul writes that we are new creations, we believe he means *now*.[4] He does not say we *will* be new creations *after* we die and go to heaven. He says that we are, present tense, new creations. Whatever Christ accomplished through his death and resurrection, it made possible the union between our spirit and the Holy Spirit.

The hope of this doctrinal distinction is beautiful. I was told as a teenager that we would always struggle with sin. While my tradition believes the struggle with sin will always be present, it would argue that we have been set free from sin's power. Meaning, we are free *not* to sin. We don't have to continuously give into willful, deliberate sin. I had never heard this perspective before, so I figured I would be destined to sin for the rest of my life. As a teenager, the struggle with lust became a real challenge. I figured I was doomed to live in defeat in this area for the rest of my life. The idea that the sanctifying power of the Holy Spirit could free me from the power of this struggle was quite liberating.

All that to say, I am a believer in the idea of sanctification and holiness. However, within the historical background of our tradition, holiness was once measured by outward conformity to a certain list of standards and rules. It has been my experience, growing up in the Christian subculture, that when holiness is measured by a certain set of standards people who meet said standards believe they have "arrived." They would

---

[4] 2 Corinthians 5:17

never say it like that. That's not humble. But internally, if they were brutally honest with themselves, they would have to admit they are a little puffed up and self-righteous.

I have come to believe that holiness cannot be measured by modified behaviors and moralistic adherence to outward standards of purity. Holiness is something that begins in the heart and works outward. You see, you can manage your behaviors without changing your heart. You can't, on the other hand, have a genuine heart change that doesn't eventually manifest in your behaviors. On one hand, this means holiness can't (and probably shouldn't) be measured. Only God knows the heart. On the other hand, the fruit or outward expression of holiness looks like love, joy, peace, patience, kindness, goodness, faithfulness, gentleness, and self-control.[5]

Jesus said that it is not what a person eats that defiles him, but what is in his heart. For us, we probably think that it is a no-brainer that food doesn't define our holiness, but for the first-century Jew what a person ate said a lot about their faithfulness to the Torah and therefore their loyalty to God. Jesus challenged their standard ways of measuring a person's holiness. He actually went a step beyond outward adherence to a list of rules. He said that what is in the heart of a person is what matters, for out of the heart come evil desires, selfishness, and dishonesty. [6]

When holiness, sanctification, and Christ-likeness is measured by outward conformity to standards it can create a false

---

[5] Galatians 5:22-23 (ESV)

[6] Matthew 15:16-20

sense of righteousness. Like I said, before having kids I thought I was fairly Christ-like. I'll go even further back in my story and confess that before marriage I thought I was fairly Christ-like. Why did I think this about myself? Because I didn't smoke, drink, cuss, or have sex with people who weren't my spouse. I was kind to people, I read Scripture regularly, and I was involved in the local church.

How did marriage change my Christ-likeness? Well, it didn't if you measure it by those standards. Marriage simply exposed things that were under the surface. My selfishness, pride, and insecurities were exposed and my self-giving love was tested. Marriage put pressure on parts of my life that other relationships allowed me to hide.

Similarly, parenting hasn't changed any of my "Christian" behaviors. Parenting has simply exposed issues of my heart—like how impatient I can be. Parenting has also exposed my faith for the weak sauce that it is. I thought I trusted God with my life before kids. Now, trusting God with my little babies is scary. I fear losing them and that fear has revealed something lacking in my trust of God.

I don't believe that I "backslid" in my faith or started living in some sort of rebellious and willful disobedience. I think my selfishness and lack of trust were there all along. They were dormant problems exposed by life's transitions. I was never truly as Christ-like as I would have liked to think. I was never as holy as my self-assessment concluded. I needed to grow in those areas before marriage and before parenthood. Marriage and parenthood simply provided the opportunity for those weaknesses to rise to the surface.

Maybe other people are more mature and godlier than I am, but I have a hunch that there are at least a few people who have experienced this too. I think most of us are actually not as good as we would like to think we are. I think many of us have found our holiness or lack of holiness exposed by life's transitions or unexpected trials.

I hold the belief that since life is constantly changing and constantly introducing new challenges to us, then we too should be constantly growing, maturing, learning, and changing. I don't think checking off a list of conservative moral standards makes you holy. I think that list can actually be a recipe for self-righteous hypocrisy. I think having a heart that is molded and conformed into the likeness of Christ is what makes you holy.

Entrenched Minds

I am writing during a time in our culture that is particularly divisive. I don't remember another time in my lifetime that has been so politically, racially, and religiously divided as now. I think what adds to this is that social media has given everyone a voice. Everyone can share their opinion. It doesn't matter if their opinion is educated and informed and true or not. If they have a Facebook or Twitter profile and a keyboard their opinion can be launched out onto the World Wide Web.

Now, I am not against people having a voice or sharing their opinions. What I have noticed though is that people can be mean. I saw a meme on Facebook that said, "Some of ya'll are too busy being Republican or Democrat to notice that you stopped being decent a long time ago." Sadly, I agree with this sentiment. I've seen some people post things online that their mom would have washed their mouths out with soap for saying in person. I suppose if people want to share their opinions and lace them with demeaning langue that is their choice, but for those us who claim to be Jesus followers, we gave up the liberty to exercise free speech in any way we want.

I presume absolutely no authority to assess a person's witness who does not claim to follow Christ by the standard of Christ. The "world" has not committed to the relational calling of following Jesus. They have not agreed to the "pick up your cross" terms of discipleship. But, if we claim to be a follower of Christ, we have agreed to the terms of followership. Not only that, if we claim Christ, we represent his name. It's like how your last name represents your family name. It's not just about you and your reputation. The reputation of your family name is on the line too. As a Christ-follower, we represent Christ.

My heart has been grieved by the ways that I have seen some Christians express themselves on social media. The dehumanizing language that is ascribed to people who have a different view or belief than they have is heartbreaking. Listen, I'm not advocating any political view or perspective here. The point is this: if we talk about people whom Christ loves in a way that is dehumanizing, hateful, judgmental, and void of compassion then we have missed the heart of Christ.

Back during the 2016 election, I shared some posts and articles on my Facebook by other thoughtful Christian leaders that raised questions concerning the election. The problem was that the questions raised challenged some of the popular views held by a large demographic of other Christians. I thought people could read something and allow it to ruminate. I thought people could thoughtfully engage views that were different from their own. I even thought people could read something, think about it, and allow their views to shift a little. At the very least, I thought people could disagree with something and remain civil.

Boy was I wrong. I was reminded very quickly that we are not very good at removing our emotional, knee-jerk responses from the equation. When our passionately held beliefs and views are challenged, it can sometimes bring out the worst in us. I actually had to remove a post because I had two Facebook friends arguing in the comment section. These friends were from different towns. They did not know each other. I removed the post because one of them, in particular, was starting to get a little hostile in their responses.

I realized that we can sometimes be really entrenched in our views. This is true of all of us to some degree or another. We like to think that we are open-minded and objective seekers of truth, but the reality is that our entrenched ways of thinking can sometimes cloud our judgment. We can often be guilty of believing this about others, but not ourselves. If you are a Democrat, you probably think Republicans are entrenched in their views and unwilling to objectively engage the facts. If you are a Republican, you think the same about the "liberal" Democrats. We tend to think our opponents are wrong and we are right. We tend to think they can't see how wrong they are because they are either just too stupid to see it or too stubborn to admit it.

The reason I bring all this up is that I think it would be helpful for all of us to embrace a little more humility. Could it be that the other side has logical and even intelligent reasons for believing what they believe? Even if they are still wrong, we would be able to win more people to our side if we began with a little more humility.

We believe what we believe because we believe it is right. There is nothing wrong with this. It is actually normal. The problem is when we hold what we believe so tightly that we are impervious to any new idea or perspective or truth. This is a problem because it lends itself to pride and pride is antithetical to growth. We can't grow if we think we have arrived. We can't learn if we think we already know. We can't be transformed if we think we're all good.

Now, I want to be clear. I am not talking about handing over for debate the core, orthodox issues of the Christian faith. I just think it is possible to hold too many views to this standard. For me, orthodoxy represents the non-negotiable truths of the Christian faith. Orthodox beliefs of the Christian faith are those truths agreed upon that transcend any single denomination, country, or historical context. The beliefs that we hold to this standard are affirmed by Christians all over the world.

Our core, orthodox beliefs should actually unify us rather than divide us.

What I have found in my time around the Church is that a lot of people take doctrinal issues—those issues about which there is some disagreement of interpretation or application within Christianity—and they make their particular brand of doctrinal issues core issues. In so doing, they ostracize all other Christ-followers who do not particularly agree with *their interpretation*.

The resurrection of Jesus is a core, orthodox belief. If someone does not believe in the resurrection, then by definition they do not believe in orthodox Christianity. Modes of baptism, style of music, or whether the pastor wears a tie when preaching are not core orthodox issues. Baptism is an important doctrinal issue, but the differences between immersion and sprinkling and infant baptism are not core, orthodox issues. The style of music and the attire of the pastor are not even in the ballpark of a doctrinal issue. Issues like that are merely subjective opinions.

My point is that there are beliefs and truths that should be held onto tightly. There are truths that should be non-negotiable. But, we should also hold onto some of our views, perspectives, and beliefs loosely enough to be teachable. We should be able to be challenged by perspectives that are different from ours or else we inhibit our own growth.

Our entrenched views can also inhibit growth by never allowing our blind spots to be exposed. We all have blind spots in our lives. We all have personality flaws and weaknesses. We all have tendencies that we are unaware of but our friends and family have identified a long time ago. My friends and family make fun of me for prefacing my conversations with long, drawn-out explanations. I explain something before I explain something. I do it all the time. I also have this tic in my neck when a shirt collar feels too tight or is tickling my neck. My wife makes fun of me for it because the tensing of my neck muscles affects my facial expression. I look quite ridiculous when I do it.

We all have blind spots and here's the thing: we don't know what we don't know. We don't know about our blind spots unless someone else helps us become aware of them. If we are too entrenched in our views, too defensive, or too prideful then people will never feel safe confronting our blind spots. Even if they do, we won't receive it well. You see, our tendency to fortify ourselves inside the walls of our own established views and perspectives actually hinders our growth.

This is also true spiritually. If we never allow people to speak truth into our lives, if we never approach a sermon with the intention of being challenged, and if we never allow the Scriptures to confront the sinful realities in our own lives then we will never change. I believe the process of being conformed into the image of Jesus is the work of the Holy Spirit. I believe transformation is like resurrection—it is God's department to work this out. However, I also believe we have to cooperate with the work of the Holy Spirit for this to happen.

God Can't

At one point during Jesus' ministry, he was in his hometown of Nazareth teaching and sharing the good news of the Kingdom. Jesus was gaining quite a reputation. He was respected as a powerful teacher by many, and the stories of his miracles circulated throughout the region. He had a reputation for being a prophet. Some of the people were really impressed with his teachings, but some of the people were offended by Jesus. Many in his hometown were skeptical because they knew him as Mary and Joseph's boy. They probably knew him as Joseph's illegitimate son.

"Who does this guy think he is to act like some special teacher or prophet?" they likely thought to themselves. Jesus tried to teach and minister there despite their attitudes, but his ministry was hindered by their lack of faith. Mark writes "He *could not* do any miracles there, except lay his hands on a few sick people and heal them."[7] In Matthew's gospel, he states it like this: "…He did not do many miracles there, *because of their unbelief.*"[8] Isn't that interesting? Jesus could not and did not do the miracles there that he had done other places because of their unbelief. *Because of their obstinate hearts, his work in their lives was hindered.*

Like the unbelieving Nazarenes, I think we can sometimes hinder God's work in our own lives. When we have these spaces in our lives that are off-limits even to God, he can't work. When we have views and perspectives and ideas

---

[7] Mark 6:5

[8] Matthew 13:58 (CSB)

that are so entrenched that not even God's Word can challenge them, we are not going grow. Paul writes that we need to be transformed by the "renewing of our minds."[9] Elsewhere he says that we need to have the "mind of Christ" and to "set our minds on things above."[10] Paul seems to believe there is an intrinsic connection between transformation and our minds. I agree with him. God often challenges how we think before he can change who we are.

When Our Views are Confronted

Not too long ago, I was reading in the book of Romans. I came to chapter 14 and found myself convicted of something I had been blind to for some time. Paul was addressing the issue of people eating certain foods or observing certain holy days. There were some Jewish Christians pointing fingers at the Gentile Christians and passing judgment on their non-Jewish behaviors. Even though they believed salvation was found in Jesus, they still had a hard time surrendering their long-held convictions about clean and unclean things.

There were some Jewish Christians in the church at Rome who were still convinced that eating certain kinds of meat was wrong and not observing the Sabbath was an offense. They believed Jesus was the Messiah and they had decided to follow Jesus, but it was still hard for them to shake off all of the Jewish laws they were brought up with.

---

[9] Romans 12:2

[10] Phil. 2:5 and Col. 3:2

There were others, especially Gentiles who had no such preexisting convictions, who believed these former ways of measuring holiness were meaningless. Paul actually says just that. He writes, "I am convinced, being fully persuaded in the Lord Jesus, that nothing is unclean in itself."[11] He even says that the person whose conscience is offended by these things has a weaker faith.

Since I have seen the pain that legalism can cause, I always loved this passage because I believed it gave me ammunition for calling out the Pharisaical legalism of other Christians. They presumed to be more holy when in fact their faith was weaker because they were still measuring their right standing with God according to adherence to certain rules. I felt justified in thinking this way, even superior. Paul tells the more conservative Christians to stop judging the others.

Scripture seemed to be on my side. The problem is that I have often had a strong disdain for those Christians I believe to be legalistic. When I read it this time, I was confronted with something that I had previously ignored. Romans 14:3 reads, "The one who eats everything must not treat with contempt the one who does not, and the one who does not eat everything must not judge the one who does, for God has accepted them." I realized I held some of my fellow believers in contempt.

Contempt describes the overall attitude of disgust we sometimes have for people who disagree with us. The more legalistic believers are told not to judge, but the believers who were living in their Christian freedom were told not to harbor

---

[11] Romans 14:14

14

contempt. I needed a heart check because I am often the Christian who holds disdain towards those rigid rule followers.

Here's the thing about becoming more like Christ—we can be right and still be wrong. We can have the right views, the right morals, the right political stances, the right doctrines, and still be wrong if we have the wrong motives and the wrong heart towards other people. Paul makes it clear that eating meat or not eating meat has little bearing on the sufficiency of Christ's death and resurrection for salvation.

However, he also makes it clear that loving one another and putting aside petty differences matters more than being right. He tells the person who eats meat to stop if it would offend one of his fellow believers. He also tells the fellow believers to stop judging the carnivores. Essentially he says, "Learn to live at peace with one another and learn how to love in the same self-giving way that Christ has loved you. That is the most important issue!" (*My paraphrase*).

We have to be willing to love those Christians that we believe are legalistic and judgmental. Conversely, we need to also love those Christians whom we believe are living a little too liberally. We don't really deal with the issue of meat sacrificed to idols, but what about someone who votes differently than you? I know Christians who vote Democrat and I know Christians who believe you can only vote Republican. I know Christians who never touch alcohol. I know people who socially partake of the fruit of the vine (i.e. alcohol). I know Christians who own guns, and I know some who believe we're called to turn our weapons into gardening tools.[12] You get the point. I think Paul would call us to love one another rather than plant another church across the street or splinter into another denomination.

I was confronted with my own lack of love for those I disagree with. In order for God to work in my heart on these blindspots, I have to first be willing to allow the Scriptures to challenge my views. If you open God's Word and everything you read already lines up with how you think then you might be missing something vital. God's Word confronts *who we are* with who God *intends for us to be*, and unless you or I have arrived there is going to be some dissonance there.

We also have to be willing to listen to other people when they call out the inconsistencies in us. My mom has called me out on this before. She has challenged me on how I have talked about other Christians. If God is going to change my heart in this area, then I have to be willing to listen to the admonition of others. I have to be willing to consider whether they might be right and I might be wrong.

Here's the thing, I'd like to think my being wrong is a rare event, but it is not. On one level or another, I am often wrong. Usually, it is my heart that needs an adjustment. Regardless of whether "they" are right or wrong, I have to look inward and examine my own heart. I cannot control the actions or views of others, but I can exercise humility in how I act or in what views I hold.

---

[12] See Isaiah 2:4 and read about Anabaptist theology

Reading this Book

I believe God wants to radically transform your life. I believe you were created to reflect the image of God and I believe you have been empowered to do so through the Holy Spirit. I believe you can look more and more like Jesus. But, I believe you have to be willing to have your views and mindsets challenged. I believe you have to consider whether it is possible that you could be wrong about some things. Even on something you have believed and held dear for a very long time.

So, as you read this book do not just take in what I write as truth. Engage with what I write and consider it carefully. I would also encourage you to notice when I say something that stirs up a defense mechanism in your mind. It will probably happen. Maybe in every chapter. I want to challenge you to not just immediately write off what I say just because you initially disagree with it. Take time to consider it. Ask yourself why such a strong defense response was triggered. Consider what it is you actually disagree with. Try to find common ground. Then, after doing this, if you still don't agree, discard the idea as wrong and foolish. Just give it a fair consideration first.

I believe some of the key areas that God wants to shape his children are in the areas of love, grace, forgiveness, and compassion. For these were revealed to be characteristic of God's self-revelation. At the cross, the grace and forgiveness and love and compassion of God as revealed in Jesus converged. Jesus is the exact representation of God. Jesus crucified is the climactic revelation of God's love for humanity, and our supreme example of Christ-likeness.

I believe that being like Jesus means we have to learn to practice grace-inspired forgiveness and compassion-motivated love. The challenge is that no one wants to be crucified. Grace-inspired forgiveness and compassion-motivated love are costly. It sounds real churchy and Christian-y, but let's be honest, we don't want to crucify our selfishness on the cross of self-giving love.

Extending grace and forgiveness to someone who doesn't deserve it is hard, more than that, it doesn't feel just. And, we often have a number of rational arguments and justifications for not doing so. Right? Having compassion for people who are different from us is counterintuitive. We are just not wired to humanize our enemies and have compassionate feelings towards them. But isn't this what Christ has called us to do? Didn't he call us to love our enemies? Didn't he model how we are to live when he declared on the cross, "Father, forgive them"? Didn't he interact with people from a place of compassion time and time again?

I believe your life and heart will be forever changed if you begin allowing God to challenge you in these areas. By his Spirit, God is able to birth a new love in your heart for people that you could never muster up on your own. I believe he can give you a new capacity to forgive people who have hurt you. It is possible for you to see even your enemies in a new way. If you believe this is possible and you want to allow God to do this in your life, then keep reading. Maybe, just maybe your views might shift just a little and that shift may create room for God to work. When that happens, the Kingdom of light defies the Kingdom of darkness.

Reflection/Discussion Questions

1. How has God worked through new stages and/or unexpected transitions to produce growth and maturity in your life? Has God ever used a season of life to expose areas of needed growth? Explain.

2. How can our narrow minded perspectives limit what God can do in our lives?

3. Anthony stated that "God often challenges how we think before he can change who we are." Do you agree or disagree with this statement? Why or why not?

4. Have you ever had something you deeply believed was true proven wrong? How did you respond?

5. How can we hold onto the core truths of our faith while at the same time cultivating a humble openness?

CHAPTER 2

What Batman Toys, Bathsheba, and Selfishness have in Common

I loved Batman growing up. I was in elementary school during the mid to late nineties when the Tim Burton and Joel Schumacher Batman movies were released. The animated series was also one of my favorite cartoons to watch. The toy companies had a hay day with these Batman movies. Especially with Batman Forever. They had all sorts of variations of Bat suits. There was "Blast Cape Batman," "Batarang Batman," and "Fireguard Batman" just to name a few. I wanted them all. (Cue the chorus of Queen's 1989 song "I Want It All").

I wanted ALL the action figures. I wanted the villains, the Batmans, the Robins, the Batcave, the Batmobile, the Batboat, and the Batwing. I am almost ashamed to admit that between birthdays, Christmas, and my own allowance money I did amount quite the collection. I say "ashamed" because I know how relentlessly I begged for toys for Christmas, and how often I got them. I was a little spoiled to say the least.

One memory in particular that stands out has to do with my sister's birthday. My younger sister looked up to me and loved playing with me. So, she played Batman with me. When we played together, she always played with the Robin action figure until we got a Batgirl. Then she was Batgirl. I was batman. I was *always* Batman. Even though Batman was my favorite, I still wanted to amass a cool collection of Robin action figures.

There was one specific Robin that I saw advertised, and I wanted it. But, my birthday wasn't for another five months. That's almost half a year! I strategically and methodically convinced my sister that she wanted said Robin for her birthday. I manipulated her into saying that she wanted it. "Wow, look at this cool Robin, it's so awesome! Wouldn't you like to play with *that?* You should ask for that for your Birthday."

So, she did. She said she wanted it for her birthday. I remember my parents encouraging me to get her something for her birthday as a kid. I "earned" an allowance for doing chores, and I was encouraged to save, tithe, and buy gifts at an early age. If I was going to get a gift for her, well, by golly it was going to benefit my interest too.

I still remember the day of her birthday party. All her little, noisy, girly friends were coming over for a slumber party. I had not gotten her a gift yet. My dad took me to Toys-R-Us to look for a gift for her. I was looking for the Robin action figure that I wanted. Toys-R-Us didn't have it. I think we went to Walmart and another store or two. We looked and looked and looked. None of the stores had that action figure. Finally, I bought a different Robin for her. Not the one I wanted and not the one I...I mean, *she* asked for.

I remember sitting in the passenger seat of our family truck and my dad saying, "Son, you ought to be ashamed of yourself."

"Why?"

"You know you aren't trying to get a gift your sister actually wants. You are looking to get this toy for yourself."

I denied it, but inside I knew he was right. I knew I was doing something tainted with selfish motives. It sunk in at the party when she opened the gift. She said "Thank you," but quickly moved on to some of the more interesting and genuine gifts from her friends and our parents. She and her girlfriends played with the toys that were more appropriate for a girl's party while the Robin got tossed aside. I realized that she was actually quite gracious, but not really as interested in the Robin toy as I was. I realized I had manipulated her and I felt remorse.

Selfishness crops up in my life quite regularly to this day. I want what I want sometimes. Or, at the very least, I don't want what would benefit others. There are days when I don't want to get up when our daughter is crying. I don't always want to play with my son. Sometimes I don't want to help with dishes, watch the kids while my wife takes time for herself, or show physical affection without sex being the end result.

Sometimes as a pastor, I don't want to rearrange my plans to meet with someone needing counsel. There are many times when I don't want to take the high road when people misunderstand my leadership decisions. Sometimes I don't want to care about other people's problems when my own personal life has its fair share of trials. Occasionally, I just don't want to put the "pastor" hat on.

The truth is this: at times I am just selfish. The Holy Spirit is quite vocal in this area of my life so I don't usually get away with it for too long. But, it is still there. My own selfish desires still show up in my life on the regular.

Selfishness unleashes so much havoc in our world. Selfishness is what motivates the company executives to pad their pockets with bonuses while draining the employee's pension plans. Selfishness is what inspires the mom to leave her husband and kids for a better "option." Selfishness is what drives the absent father to invest more in his job than his family. Selfishness closes the heart off to generous compassion and ignores the plight of the poor. Selfishness contributes to the struggle with addiction. Selfishness ruins relationships. Selfishness obstructs the free flow of God's love to us and through us. We know that selfishness causes obvious problems. Yet, even though we know this, many of us still act selfishly from time to time.

Selfish Self Care?

Have you ever flown? If you have then you know the little safety spiel that the flight attendants go through before takeoff. You know that if the cabin loses pressure, the oxygen masks will drop down. They always advise that you secure yours *first* before helping someone else. Why? Because you're not any help to anyone else if you're passed out. I know this might be an overused illustration, but it is true. We cannot give to others what we do not have. We cannot give selflessly to others if we have nothing in our tanks to give.

Self-care is a hot topic these days. I am sure that there are times when this can be out of balance in a person's life. However, I have also experienced the burnout that comes from not tending to my own spiritual, mental, emotional, and physical health. Self-care is not selfish unless it completely displaces acts of self-giving love. Self-care can actually be a self-giving act if it has the goal to love others in mind. I monitor my emotional, physical, and spiritual health *so that* I have something to offer my family and the people I minister to.

I believe it is important that we understand what selfishness *is not* before we talk about what it is. It is not selfish to take time to spend in God's presence, to rest, to exercise, to go on vacation, or to reflect. It is also not selfish to sometimes say "no" to the church. Why? Because every "yes" is actually a "no" to something else. I was talking with someone the other day that felt the need to apologize because she couldn't serve in some particular way due to important family plans that were already established. She shouldn't have to apologize for that. Investing in one's family is important. Even biblical.

Selfishness is not a healthy embrace of self-care. Selfishness is being consumed with your own interests for your own sake. Selfishness is manipulating other people in your life so that you get what you want. Selfishness is seeing things only your way. Selfishness is always saying "yes" to your self-care and never saying "yes" to serving others. Selfishness is looking out for your own interests at the expense of others. Selfishness is disregarding the perspective, plight, and position of others.

When I think of selfishness displayed in the Scriptures, I think of David. That's right. King David. The greatest, most beloved King of Israel. The author of over 70 of the Psalms. The one who is said to have been a man after God's own heart. One of his most epic moral failures was, among other things, an act of selfishness.

Ooh La-la

It was the spring of the year, after the rainy season in the Middle East when nations resumed their military campaigns. Joab, David's military general, was sent with an army of warriors to settle some scores on behalf of the nation. Meanwhile, David settled into the comfort of the palace in Jerusalem.

David had spent a good part of his life up to this point on the run and engaging in war. He had served his time and earned his glory—he's a giant-slayer for Pete's sake! Why not take a load off and enjoy the office of king? Besides, Joab was a capable military leader.

In that culture and even in a number of cultures today, it was normative to take a midday nap. One evening, after David had awakened from his afternoon nap, he took a stroll on the palace terrace. As he breathed in the cool evening air his eyes caught a glimpse of something—something he was designed and wired to take delight in. Something he could hardly look away from. From his palace terrace, he saw a woman bathing. The woman is described as being "very beautiful"—the Hebrew words used here are the same words used in Genesis describing all that God had made.[13] Bathsheba was a woman whose physical appearance was "very good" with an emphasis on "very." In other words, she was gorgeous.

David didn't sin by seeing this woman. Maybe he accidentally on purpose saw her. Maybe he had seen this woman before by complete accident but now knew where her house was and when she bathed. Maybe he didn't. David's sin wasn't that he saw a woman and noticed she was beautiful—the text lets us know that you would have to have been blind not to notice. David's sin was conceived when he began entertaining the idea of taking for himself what was not rightfully his. Sin was conceived when David began conspiring a way to exploit another human being for his own pleasure.

The New Testament author, James, writes, "Temptation comes from our own desires, which entice us and drag us away. These desires give birth to sinful actions. And when sin is allowed to grow, it gives birth to death."[14] Our own, selfish desires can drag us away to places we never would have gone before. Selfishness can grow inside us, metastasize, and give birth to something that will kill us!

David finds out who she is, sends his messengers to retriever her, so that she can be brought to the palace. Whether Bathsheba was complicit or not is not really the point. Her name implies she is actually not an Israelite by blood, but rather a sojourner. Her husband was Uriah "the Hittite." If she was a

---

[13] Genesis 1:31

[14] James 1:14-15 (NLT)

Hittite and not an Israelite by blood, then she was a foreigner in a land that was not her home. This reality alone affected her status. Not only that, she was also a woman in a male-dominated culture. Women were practically property. In addition to that, there's also the fact that David was the King—a divine monarch. She was a female foreigner with absolutely no position to deny the king's request. The fact of the matter is: David used his position to seize that which was not his, and then after he exploited what he wanted, he sent her away.

It is easy for us to view this as a horrible sin, but, this would not have been that frowned upon by other Ancient Near Eastern monarchs. David was a king and he had a divine right to whatever he wanted—especially if it was already under the authority of his reign! No one—at least none of David's contemporaries—would have blamed David for what he did. In fact, some would maybe say he was entitled to it. He was the king.

That's the thing about selfishness. The world often doesn't blame us for taking what is rightfully ours, getting even, or putting ourselves first. "You gotta look out for number one." Right? We have all sorts of ways that we rationalize, justify, and compromise. We appeal to the approval of others and often we find that no one blames us. Yet, as with David, God is not pleased.

A month or so goes by and Bathsheba sends word that she's pregnant and her husband is still away at war. David's sin is about to be made public. So, he conceived a plan. (Pun intended.) He called for Joab to send Uriah home to bring a report from the battlefield. When Uriah arrived, David made small talk with him for a while and then encouraged him to go home, relax, and enjoy his wife. No harm, no foul as they say. Right? Uriah left the palace, but he didn't go home. Instead, he slept at the gate of the palace.

The next morning David found out his plan didn't work. He asks Uriah, "Why didn't you go home?" Uriah's response is a cutting indictment against David, "The Ark and the armies of Israel and Judah are living in tents, and Joab and my master's men are camping in the open fields. How could I go home to wine and dine and sleep with my wife? I swear that I would never do such a thing."[15]

David made one more attempt to get Uriah to go home to his wife. He got him drunker than a skunk thinking he'd stumble home and sleep with his wife. In spite of his intoxication, Uriah again slept at the gate. What David did next is low. David sent Uriah back to the battlefield with his own death sentence in hand. Uriah journeyed back to the battlefield carrying a message to Joab that instructed Joab to place him where the fighting was fiercest and then pull back.

David's plan seemed to have worked. Uriah was killed on the battlefield. David allowed Bathsheba time to mourn her dead husband, but then he swiftly took her to be his wife. At this point in the story, the whole ordeal seems to be settled and no one is none the wiser. But, the 11th chapter of 2 Samuel ends like this: "But the Lord was displeased with what David had done."[16]

---

[15] 2 Samuel 11:11 (NLT)

[16] 2 Samuel 11:27 (NLT)

So God sent a prophet named Nathan. Many times when we see the word "prophet" we have in mind this idea of a fortuneteller. That's not really what a prophet was or is. Prophets are simply individuals called by God to proclaim the truth of God. They were preachers, and preachers are annoying. (Can I get an amen?) They have this tendency to talk about things and address things and point out things that you don't want to talk about, address, or have pointed out. And, they often do it by weaving God's truth into a story.

So, Nathan approached David and told him a story about a rich man and a poor man. The rich man had a number of sheep and cattle, and truth be told he could have acquired more if he wanted. The poor man, on the other hand, had one little ewe lamb. This lamb was more than livestock to him. This lamb was a pet, and as you know pets have a way of becoming part of the family. This lamb shared his food, drank from his cup and even slept in his arms. He loved this lamb as if it were his own child.

On one occasion, the rich man had to show hospitality to a guest, but he didn't want it to cost him anything. So he crossed the boundary into his neighbor's pasture and took his neighbor's only lamb, slaughtered it, and entertained his guest giving the appearance that he was sacrificially hospitable. The rich man had taken advantage of his neighbor. Justice demands the situation be made right. It was not entirely unusual for David to decide, as the king, what should be done in civil cases. Looking David in the eyes, Nathan asks what must be done to right the situation.

David was enraged by the injustice in the story. Have you ever heard about something or witnessed something happen that was so unfair, so unjust that it felt like your blood was literally boiling? Have you ever been enraged by injustice? Have ever known of something that happened to another person that was so wrong that every just, right, and true bone in your body cried out for something to be done?

That is how David felt. He declared, "This man deserves to die." His initial reaction was a little harsh. Truth be told, David knew his offense was not a capital offense. The "deserves to die" part was his emotional reaction, but the real verdict David decided was that, "He must pay for that lamb four times over because he did such a thing and had no pity."

Nathan, with piercing poignancy, looked David in the eyes and said, "You are the man."

It's like the eyes of David's heart were opened, and for the first time in the entire narrative, he saw the horrific nature of his actions. He saw clearly how much pain he had caused. You see, our selfish sin always unleashes a ripple effect of brokenness that touches the lives of other people, and oftentimes, the lives of those we love most. *Even those sins that we think are private have a way of warping the image of God imprinted on our souls in such a way that we can no longer accurately see the image of God in others and therefore, we can no longer relate rightly with God or others.*

Selfish Crime

Our selfishness is not a victimless sin. Our selfishness almost always hurts other people. Several years ago, my wife and I were car hunting. Craig's List has always been a little shady, but once upon a time its "shady factor" was lower on the scale. We found a mid-2000s Audi on Craig's List for under $5k. We emailed to inquire about the price of the car. The story we received was that the car belonged to this lady's son, but he was killed in a motorcycle accident not long ago. She just wanted to get rid of the car because it was a constant reminder of her son.

We shared our condolences for her loss, but proceeded to communicate that we were also interested in the car. She said she lived out of state but she could send the car to us through eBay. We could test drive the car for a couple of days and decide if we wanted it. All we would have to do is send a deposit via a MoneyGram to a lawyer who wouldn't release the money unless the purchase was finalized. (Are you seeing the red flags our naïve selves missed?) She said we would receive an email from eBay verifying the process. Which, we did. The email header looked as if it was from eBay. Our young, somewhat newlywed selves thought the whole thing was legit.

We sent a sizable deposit, but the car never came. Surprise, surprise. When I received an email saying inclement weather (in the middle of the summer) had prohibited the tractor-trailer from leaving and more funds were needed, I became suspicious. Just a quick search on Google revealed that one of the red flags of a scam is when another site outside of eBay claims to use some of eBay's features. eBay does not serve as a shipping company or an escrow company, and other sites cannot use eBay's protection plans—just in case you were wondering.[17]

We were duped. It was a good lesson learned the hard way. What saddens me is the utter selfishness of the thief/thieves. We were out a good chunk of money that took us a long time to save up. Remember, we were young newlyweds and I am a pastor. It's not like we have a lot of disposable income just laying around. I went to the police, but the case was likely never a priority. We lost the money to someone who had the nerve to conjure up a story about their deceased son. They manipulated us and would have continued to try to get more money out of us with absolutely no concern for the impact it would have on our lives. That is our "we've been scammed" story, but thousands of people have been scammed, hacked, robbed, and manipulated.

Selfishness is expensive. It harms others, and actions that harm others are often inherently selfish. A Psychology Today author commented on selfishness writing, "Virtually all behavior that intentionally harms other people is rooted in the perpetrators' beliefs that their own desires are so much more important than other people's that they are entitled to rob, scam, cheat, and hurt others in order to get what they want. "[18] Think about that. Most harmful behaviors begin by

---

[17] "EBay Motors–Purchase Protection–Overview." n.d. Pages.ebay.com. https://pages.ebay.com/motors/buy/purchase-protection/.

[18] Leary, M. (2017, September 11). The Scourge of Selfishness. Retrieved July 15, 2020, from https://www.psychologytoday.com/us/blog/toward-less-egoic-world/201709/the-scourge-selfishness

us thinking we are more important than other people. Most harmful behaviors are fundamentally selfish.

Our actions and behaviors that hurt other people are rarely rooted in our good intentions. Sometimes we have good intentions but have flawed execution. Other times though, we are just plain selfish and our selfishness has consequences.

Gimme Hands

A couple of weeks ago, I was in my son's room and I saw a book on the floor titled *Buzzle Billy*. As I opened it, my memories were triggered and I remembered the book being a story my grandma had read to me. She had gifted it to us to pass on to our kids. *Buzzle Billy* is a children's fable about sharing.

Billy was a Buzzle. Buzzles lived in a land where all the buildings were made out of puzzles. Buzzles really liked to play. "They road Buzz-carts, they played Buzz-darts, they went on hikes, they rode their bikes, and on and on and on they played 'til something happened one sad day!" When Billy saw a boy playing with his favorite toy he shouted, "That's mine! Gimme that!" What happened next was quite unexpected, Buzzle Billy popped out a third hand.

You see, "When Buzzles turned to selfishness, it got them in an awful mess, each time they reached for something new, POP! A brand-new hand just grew!" As the story goes on, Billy just keeps grabbing toys from other boys and girls. As he grabs more toys, more "Gimme hands" appear. At first, it seems like an asset. I mean, he has all these extra hands to play with all the cool toys. But, all the other children start to run away from "Gimme Hand Billy." At first, he was content to not have anyone else to play with:

Now Buzzle Billy laughed with glee,
"All these toys belong to me!
They are mine! I will not share!
Mine! Mine! Mine! I won't play fair"

Now that all his friends were gone
Buzzle Billy sat alone.
He sat and played all by himself,
All alone…
With no one else.
And soon he thought, "This is no fun,
I need a friend; I'll go find one.
I'll make a friend, but I won't share.
I'll keep my toys, and they'll keep theirs."

His efforts to make a friend were unsuccessful. He wanted to have his cake and eat it too. He wanted friends but he didn't want to share. One day, as he sat crying, a girl came up to Billy. She asked him what was wrong. He shared that all his friends were gone. The girl offered to play with Billy, and her kindness softened Billy's heart. When she asked if she could play with his teddy bear, he gave it to her. You know what happened next? One of his hands disappeared.

The cure for "Gimme Hands" was to share with others and give away the amassed toys. Buzzle Billy shouted for all the other boys and girls to come share his toys. "The more he shared, the more they cheered, his Gimme hands all disappeared! The Buzzle children laughed and played and many, many friends were made."

This fun little story reveals a number of truths about selfishness. One of which is that selfishness always leads to isolation. When we think only of ourselves, we will eventually have only ourselves to think of. In this way, other people are not the only victims of our selfishness. Our selfishness also hurts us. Our selfishness can cause people to avoid deep friendship with us. Our selfishness can push people away and create rifts in our relationships.

We were created for relationship and community. We do not thrive in isolation. So the paradox of wholeness is this: those who promote themselves first will be last and those who give their life away will find life. (Sounds like something Jesus said…) We are most whole when we are loving others well because it is only in giving love that we also receive love. Buzzle Billy could not have fun playing with friends when he played alone. As he shared with his friends, his fun was expanded. As we give love to others, we experience the goodness of love in return. When we love only ourselves, love can only be reciprocated with ourselves.[19]

---

[19] Michael P. Waite and Jill Trousdale, *Buzzle Billy: a Book about Sharing* (Chariot Books, 1987)

Turning Point

Have you ever found yourself in a place where everything looked good on the outside, but in your soul you kept asking: "Oh God, what have I done... who have I become?" This was the state of David's heart after Nathan's confrontation. I want to point out that it was through the proclamation of God's truth by another person that David's eyes were opened. Certainly the Holy Spirit convicts us of our sin, but at the same time, we have an infinite ability to be self-deceived. We have an infinite ability to rationalize and justify our actions. Sometimes, we need someone else to speak the truth we need to hear. That, in part, is why being part of a community of believers that also gathers to listen to the Word of God proclaimed is so important.

When David's sin was confronted, and he was faced the reality of his selfish actions, he was moved to repentance. Psalm 51 is one of the Psalms attributed to David and is a song of repentance. David's sin with Bathsheba is the background of the psalm and his interaction with Nathan the inspiration. David wrote,

> *Have mercy on me, O God,*
> *according to your unfailing love;*
> *according to your great compassion*
> *blot out my transgressions.*
> *Wash away all my iniquity*
> *and cleanse me from my sin.*

For I know my transgressions,
and my sin is always before me.
Against you, you only, have I sinned
and done what is evil in your sight;
so you are right in your verdict
and justified when you judge.
Surely I was sinful at birth,
sinful from the time my mother conceived me.
Yet you desired faithfulness even in the womb;
you taught me wisdom in that secret place.

Create in me a pure heart, O God,
and renew a steadfast spirit within me.
Do not cast me from your presence
or take your Holy Spirit from me.
Restore to me the joy of your salvation
and grant me a willing spirit, to sustain me.[20]

For so many of us, our tendency when we realize our sin is to retreat from God—to avoid him. Notice David's response. David pursued God because David knew something about God that we often misunderstand. David knew that God is a God of unfailing love and great compassion. David approached God pleading for mercy and forgiveness. He poetically asked God to forgive his sin by asking God to blot it out or erase his sin, to wash it like a garment, and to purify it like metal. Blot, wash, purify.

---

[20] Psalm 51:1-6; 10-12

David continued to acknowledge something deeply profound. He stated that he had sinned against God, and God alone. This statement should not be understood as David dismissing the atrocities of his sin against Bathsheba, Uriah, and the nation of Israel. Rather, David was acknowledging that to sin against God's children, who bear his image, is to sin against God. Don't be mistaken. When we sin—whether in word, thought or deed—against one of God's beloved, we have grieved God's heart and sinned against him.

David further acknowledged that the issue was not just about this isolated event, this one instance where he had a lapse in judgment, or this one moment of indiscretion. The problem isn't just his actions or his behaviors. No. It's not that simple. The problem is his heart. He was born wrong. There is something dreadfully wrong with his heart.

So many of us have bought into one of two lies. Some of us have been raised in a tradition that taught us that our sin is so horrific and repulsive to God that he can hardly stand the sight of us. This couldn't be further from the truth! It is an affront to God's glory and faithful love to believe our sin is greater than the reach of his love. Jesus thought you worth dying for. He loves you with an everlasting love. You don't take on flesh, die on a cross, and rise from the dead to reconcile a world you despise. God loves you. He always has, and he always will.

Some of us have bought into the lie on the other extreme. Some of us don't really take sin seriously. We have bought into the narrative that believes humans are basically good. We're not that bad. There are just a few bad eggs, but not everyone is that sinful. Especially not you. The truth is that God loves us enough to take upon himself the weight of our collective sin and provide a way for our redemption. Sin is a big deal, but it has not and it will not diminish God's resolve to break the power of sin's hold on us.

David asked for forgiveness, but then he asked for something much more profound. He asked God to create in him a pure heart. The word "create" is the Hebrew word bara (*baw-raw*).[21] This word is the same word used in Genesis describing the creation of the cosmos out of nothing. This word, when used in reference to creating, is always used with God as the subject. "Bara" creation is the kind of creation that only God can do. "Bara" creation is transformative, out-of-nothing creation.

Some Christians seem to think that all God has wanted to do is to make us nice. That salvation was about a ticket to heaven and holiness was about sin management. God doesn't want to make us nice, God is not interested in how well we manage our sin issues or modify our behaviors, and God isn't interested in whether we smoke or drink as if outward actions were the only measure of a clean heart. This is not try-harder-be-a-good-person-avoid-beer-and-sex theology.

This is resurrection!

God is interested in giving us a new *bara'* heart. God is interested in the life, the mind, the heart, and the will of Christ actually being fully formed in us. God is interested in doing a

---

[21] "H1254–bārā'–Strong's Hebrew Lexicon (kjv)." Blue Letter Bible. Accessed 9 Sep, 2022. https://www.blueletterbible.org/lexicon/h1254/kjv/wlc/0-1/.

work in our souls that is so radical and so unprecedented that the only thing that could parallel its magnitude is if someone who was dead walked out of his grave!

When we believe this is the sort of thing God is up to, it opens a whole new world of transformative possibilities. We may struggle with sin and selfishness, but we never resign ourselves to defeat. We never accept that "This is just who I am" or "It's just my personality." We continually believe and expect God to change our hearts. Resurrection is God's work, but the pathway to crucifying our old selves is repentance.

Repentance simply means to turn, to change directions. The change of direction involves a couple of things on our part. Changing directions means a change of mind concerning the destination. It means thinking differently about where we are going and how we are getting there. Part of how we start to think differently is by acknowledging our selfish sin and confessing it. We can't hide it, deny it, or normalize it. We have to acknowledge it and admit that it is sin. It's not just an "oops" or a "mistake." We have to admit that our selfish actions are sin.

The other aspect of repentance involves action. Changing directions requires movement that is oriented towards another destination. We cannot keep doing the things that are leading us in one direction if we are heading towards another. Repentance means exchanging our way of thinking about life for God's way, and then aligning our lives accordingly.

Part of the human condition is that we are selfish. It's part of our nature. But, thank God, he can change our very nature. In fact, Jesus' death and resurrection already purchased our new identities. We have to come to the end of ourselves and actually desire for God to do a work that progressively puts our selfishness to death. As we allow Christ to change our hearts, he plants the seeds of his love in our hearts. As those seeds blossom and mature, we find that we have a new capacity to love others. The greater our capacity to love others, the smaller our capacity to love only ourselves.

Reflection/Discussion Questions

1. Have you ever been hurt by someone else's selfishness? Without harboring resentment for the person, can you describe the harmful effects of selfishness?

2. How does selfishness show up in your own actions sometimes?

3. Describe the difference between self-care and selfishness.

4. We talk a lot about repentance in the Church. In your own words, explain what repentance is and how we are transformed by it.

5. Anthony suggested that a key piece of repentance is acknowledging our selfishness as sin. Why is it so important that we address sin by first acknowledging it?

CHAPTER 3

Foot Work

I t was the day before the Teacher would give his life for the sins of the world. The week had been a whirlwind. Jerusalem was a buzz as thousands of Israelites from all over the world had made their pilgrimage to celebrate the Passover festival. Passover always brings a population influx to the city, but this year the atmosphere was a little different. Passover commemorates God's deliverance of Israel from slavery in Egypt. God acted decisively and miraculously to deliver Israel from oppression. The word on the street was that God was about to act again through this prophet-rabbi from the backwoods of Nazareth.

Hopes were high that this demon-exorcising, dead-raising prophet was Israel's long hoped for Messiah. Sunday, as Jesus entered the city, Roman soldiers who were dispatched to keep peace during the festival watched on as people heralded Jesus as a king. They shouted, "Hosanna to the Son of David. Blessed is he who comes in the name of the Lord! Hosanna in the highest heaven!"[22] Hosanna means "save, we pray." The

---

[22] Matthew 21:9

implication was clear: Jesus is being ushered into the city of Jerusalem during the Passover festival as the Messiah—who they believed would be a military and political revolutionary.

Thursday evening Jesus sat down for a meal with his disciples. Luke tells us that at some point during the course of the evening, the disciples began to argue about who of them was the greatest.[23] Perhaps they were arguing about where they were going to sit since the seating arrangements in that culture indicated one's importance. They likely jockeyed for position and power because they believed their status would carry over into the coming Kingdom. They wanted seats of honor and power once Jesus led Israel to victory over Rome and established his Kingdom.

While they were arguing over power and honor, Jesus covertly gets up from the table. By the time the disciples notice, they are startled by what they see. Jesus has taken off his outer garment, and is shamefully dressed down to the attire of a slave! Not only that, he had wrapped a towel around his waist and was pouring water into a basin.

What Jesus does next is nothing short of astonishing. During that time, they would recline at the table leaning on their left arm and eating from the table with their right, their feet facing outward. Jesus, dressed like a slave and carrying the water basin, stoops and washes the disciple's feet one by one.

The roads were filthy, full of animal and human excrement. Since people wore sandals, you can probably imagine their feet being extremely dirty. It was a customary act of hospitality for

---

[23] Luke 22:24

the host to at least provide a basin of water for guests to wash their feet, and often times a lower ranking servant or slave would wash the guest's feet. But one would never wash the feet of another unless they were the other's inferior. One author suggests, "Footwashing could be used as a synonym for slavery. To wash another's feet symbolized the subjugation of one person to another. Those who received footwashing from another were social superiors of those who performed the task."[24]

John adds to the context of this humiliating act by noting a couple of things that were on Jesus' mind. John tells us that Jesus knew the time had come for his sacrificial death and he knew he was going back to the Father. In other words, Jesus knew the gravity of what was about to take place and the suffering he was about to endure. He also knew *who* he was. He knew he was God. He knew he was in fact the greatest among them. He was superior. He was not just "rabbi" or "master" or even "lord" with a lower case "l." He was God. He also knew Judas had already agreed to betray him.

Yet, he stooped.

He laid aside his garment to take on the most humiliating form possible in that setting.

And, he washed their feet. Even the feet of Judas.

John introduces this whole scene by stating, "Having loved his own who were in the world, he loved them to the end."[25]

---

[24] Thomas, John Christopher. (1991) *Footwashing in John 13 and the Johannine Community* as quoted http://www.zionlutherannj.net/foot-washing-in-the-old-and-new-testament-the-graeco-roman-world-the-early-church-and-the-liturgy-2/#_ftn5.

[25] John 13:1

John's statement is of course a foreshadowing of Jesus' ultimate sacrifice on the cross, but it is no insignificant detail that he foreshadows the cross by expressing Christ's self-giving love in this scene. Jesus demonstrates with this sign act what self-giving love looks like. Jesus stoops to serve others, even others who would be responsible for inflicting significant pain. Jesus stoops. Jesus serves. Jesus loves.

Love to Give

Love is a weird thing. We seem to have a fundamental human need for it. So many of our identity crises are rooted in our attempt to answer the question: Am I loveable? We look for validation in all sorts of places. We seem prone to living as if our accomplishments, accolades, and salaries validate our worth. Like, if we just secure that promotion or earn that dollar amount it will prove that we matter. If we matter, then we are loveable.

I was talking with a young professional one time who essentially admitted this. He had a certain dollar amount in his mind that he expected himself to earn. That dollar amount was a sort of validation. In order to pursue that dollar amount he worked a lot of hours. He was a new dad though and his workaholism was starting to collide with his desire to be present as a dad.

For me, this search for love has created a deep aversion to failure. I fear failure because to fail would undermine my value. So, I got good grades in school, I try to preach good sermons, and I help with the dishes at home. None of these things are inherently bad. The problem is when I anchor my value in my performance.

Many of us learn at a young age that we need to earn our value. In my ministry experience, I have encountered so many people who have wounds that were inflicted by something a parent did or said to them when they were young. The question of their value was either left unanswered, or answered negatively. For many, the wound haunts them well into adulthood. Consequently, their search for love has taken them down heartbreaking paths.

We live from a place of needing love, desiring love, and craving love. But, this is where the mysterious nature of love is exposed. Because, as much as we need it, we can't forcefully acquire it. If we go after it, if we try to grasp at it, if we try to seize it, it seems to allude us. We can't force love out of other people. Love must be given. Love must be freely chosen.

When we try to take love, it turns into something other than love. When we impose our need for love on other people we distort and disfigure the relationship. We enslave the other person to our wants, needs, and desires. At that point, the relationship becomes abusive and toxic. It becomes selfish to the core, no longer recognizable as love.

So we are left with this predicament: We need love, but we can't coerce it or force it. Not only that, as Christ-followers, we are called to love others as Christ loves us. We are called to give something away that we ourselves desperately need.

In his book *Blue like Jazz*, Donald Miller talks about attending a lecture in which a communications professor spoke about the power of metaphor. He experimented with the group by sharing a word or concept and then asking what metaphors are associated with stated topic. When he brought up the topic of relationships the group suggested metaphors like "we *value* people," "we *invest* in people," "people are *priceless*," and a "relationship can be *bankrupt*." Miller notes that almost all of the metaphors shared were economic metaphors. He writes,

> ...we think of love as a commodity. We use it like money. ....If someone is doing something for us, offering us something, be it gifts, time, popularity, or what have you, we feel they have value, we feel they are worth something to us, and, perhaps, we feel they are priceless....I was guilty of using love like money, withholding it to get somebody to be who I wanted them to be. I was making a mess of everything. And I was disobeying God. I became convicted about these things, so much so that I had some trouble getting sleep. It was clear that I was to love everybody, be delighted at everybody's existence, and I had fallen miles short of God's aim.[26]

When love is transactional, we will do cost-benefit analysis to determine whether other people are worth loving. Our

---

[26] Donald Miller, *Blue Like Jazz* (Nashville: Thomas Nelson, 2003), 218-220.

love may even be dependent on whether we will receive love in return.

This is problematic when we are called to love others as Christ loved us. Jesus gave up his life for us. That is a high standard for others-oriented love. Not only that, we have a human need for love. How can we love others in a self-giving way that is not concerned with our own need for love being met?

Rest In Love

Jesus wasn't jockeying for position to secure his value or need for love in part because he was God. But, Jesus being God doesn't let us off the hook. We are called to follow and imitate him. Jesus shows us what it means to live authentically human and spiritually whole. So, what secret did Jesus know that allowed him to be free from competing for value?

He knew he was loved by his Father. Before Jesus started his ministry, he went to John the Baptizer to be baptized. Baptism was a symbolic act that represented cleansing from sin. When Jesus was baptized, it was the first time he identified with us. In a symbolic way, he took upon himself the weight of our sin at his baptism.

After John dunked Jesus and lifted him out of the water something peculiar happened. The heavens opened and the Holy Spirit fell upon Jesus in the form of a dove. There was also a voice from heaven that declared, "This is my *beloved* Son, with whom I am well pleased."[27] Before Jesus had taught a single word, cast out a single demon, or healed a single

---

[27] Matthew 3:17 ESV

person—before his ministry had begun and before he had performed a single miracle—God's love rested on him.

Jesus didn't concern himself with status and honor and value estimates because he was secure in his Father's love. We too, by the power of his Spirit, can come to a place where we are confident of his love for us. Henri Nouwen wrote, "Self-rejection is the greatest enemy of the spiritual life because it contradicts the sacred voice that calls us the 'Beloved.' Being the Beloved expresses the core truth of our existence."[28]

Just in case you think I am making too much of God's love, just read what Paul wrote to the Galatians:

> But when the right time came, God sent his Son, born of a woman, subject to the law. God sent him to buy freedom for us who were slaves to the law, so that he could *adopt* us as his very own *children*. And because we are his children, God has sent the Spirit of his Son into our hearts, prompting us to call out, 'Abba, Father.' Now you are no longer a slave but God's own child. And since you are his child, God has made you his heir.[29]

We are God's children. I am a parent and this concept of being God's child hits me differently in this season of life. I can't really explain it. All I can say is that I love my children

---

[28] Henry Nouwen, *Life of the Beloved* (New York: The Crossroad Publishing Company, 1992), 33.

[29] Galatians 4:4-7 (NLT)

with a love that is unlike any other love I have for any other human relationship I have. If that is how God loves us, then I can rest in his love. I don't have to try to prove my value.

Here is the beautiful truth: When our need for love is eternally satisfied by the God who is eternal love, we can be free to love others with abandon. When we don't have to prove our value or worth, our love stops needing to be a transaction where we are concerned about balancing the scales. When we are not starving for love and value, we no longer need to tax the people we are in relationship with.

When we begin love others without expecting a love deposit from them, our love becomes what love was truly intended to be. So often our love is polluted with our selfishness that our entire concept of love becomes distorted. Love, by nature, is others oriented. Love gives itself away. It can't help but give. When we begin loving people freely, it is then that we truly begin to love.

I will again quote Henri Nouwen, "Our humanity comes to its fullest bloom in giving. We become beautiful people when we give whatever we can give…"[30] We were made for relationships of love by a Creator who is, within himself, a relationship of love. Therefore, we are most truly human, in the sense that we most reflect the Divine image we were created in, when we give love.

The mysterious thing about giving love is that the economy of the Kingdom confounds the economy of the world. In giving love, we often find that we receive love. Jesus taught that it is

---

[30] Nouwen, *Life of the Beloved*, 106.

more blessed to give than receive.[31] I think when we give love it has a way of changing the environment because the atmosphere becomes characterized by giving. A self-giving atmosphere creates an environment where people are free to love as God does.

We can't force, coerce, or exact love out of other people to fulfill our own need for love. We can only rest in God's love and give love away. When we do, a supernatural exchange takes.

Supernatural Exchange

Resting in God's love is something that I believe happens in our interior lives—in our souls. Giving love to others is something that is lived outwardly through action. Jesus, for example, knew he was loved by God, and his giving of love was demonstrated through action. He got up from the table, assumed a lowly position, and washed the disciple's feet. It was an outward action that demonstrated Jesus' inward humility.

We need love, so giving it away is counterintuitive. But, resting in God's love makes it possible for us to give it away. Resting in God's love frees us from fighting for our value and from trying to love others conditionally. After our interior lives are rooted in God's love, we can begin to grow in loving others, but we actually have to cooperate with the Holy Spirit to live it out. We need the Holy Spirit's help to love others *and* demonstrate it.

The act of giving love away is an act of faith that is empowered by the Spirit, because the act of giving love away requires

---

[31] Acts 20:35

the denial of self. The Holy Spirit works to transform us, but the Holy Spirit doesn't live out that transformation for us. We have to cooperate. We have to lean into the Holy Spirit's work. In other words, we actually have to be intentional. The Holy Spirit transforms us, but we have to walk out that transformation on purpose with purpose. In order to love in a self-giving way, we have to defy our selfishness.

Living out the self-giving, others-oriented love that God calls us to demands that we sometimes, as Jesus did, set aside the garment of our pride so that we can humbly serve others. And, that is hard. I am not naturally prone to setting aside my selfish pride. The Spirit helps us and transforms us, but the hard work of denying ourselves so that the Spirit can work is still necessary.

Self-Awareness

I think part of our cooperation in the transformation process begins with awareness. Awareness is the first step to a new mindset. We have to be aware of the things in our hearts and minds that conflict with Christ before we can ask him to change them. Our awareness reveals our deep need for God to transform us. The Holy Spirit awakens us to certain things that need to be changed in our hearts.

One of the things he will awaken in us is our awareness of our own selfishness. Our awareness of our own selfishness will not eradicate it. We may still act in self-centered ways, but we will know it. We will experience the conviction of the Holy Spirit in that area of our lives. We will know we need to repent.

Repentance is an act of self-denial as it forces us to exchange our way for God's way.

Awareness creates room for conviction, conviction leads us to repentance, and repentance invites God to change us. Many of us do not experience the transformation in our lives that God wants to do because we are not even aware of our own blind spots. We don't know what we don't know, and sometimes, we don't know that we need God to transform our blind areas.

There are a couple of ways that our blind spots can become exposed. One is through other people—especially those people who know us and love us. They often see things in our hearts and behaviors that others do not. Another way is through Scripture. Sometimes the Holy Spirit will magnify a passage you are reading or use a sermon to convict you. I also believe we can learn of areas that need transformed as we intentionally practice self-awareness and reflection. As we become increasingly aware of the things God needs to change, the simplest act of cooperation we can do is invite him to do what only he can do. We can ask God to transform us.

When we ask God to do things that he already wants to do in us, I believe he does. It may happen in a radically transformative moment or it may gradually happen over a period of time. Some people experience what I call "growth spurt transformations"—their growth is really fast and dramatic. For others, they have long seasons of transformational growth. The point is, when we ask God to change us, he will.

As you recognize the sin of your selfishness and repent of it, God will forgive you and cleanse you. He will change you. As you recognize that some of your selfish actions are really rooted in your deficiency of love, God will remind you of his love. As you rest in his love, you will find that you have a new capacity to love others. Then, when we love other people in self-giving ways, we defy the selfishness and pride and insecurities that inhibit God's love from flowing freely through us to others.

I believe the most appropriate way to end this chapter would be to end with the words of Paul and the Philippian hymn:

> Do nothing out of selfish ambition or vain conceit.
> Rather, in humility value others above yourselves,
> not looking to your own interests but each of you
> to the interests of the others.

> In your relationships with one another, have the
> same mindset as Christ Jesus:

> Who, being in very nature God, did not consider
> equality with God something to be used to his
> own advantage; rather, he made himself nothing
> by taking the very nature of a servant, being made
> in human likeness. And being found in appear-
> ance as a man, he humbled himself by becoming
> obedient to death—even death on a cross![32]

---

[32] Philippians 2: 3-8

Have the same mindset as Christ. Do not look to your own interests. Imitate Christ's humility, and in so doing, you will imitate his self-giving, others-oriented love.

Reflection/Discussion Questions

1. What characteristics of self-giving love do you see Jesus demonstrating when he washes the disciple's feet in John 13:1-17?

2. In what ways might we treat love like a transaction?

3. How does our own need for love sometimes hijack our ability to love others in self-giving ways?

4. What does it mean to "rest in God's love" and how might that free us to love others more truly?

5. Anthony suggested that growth looks like becoming aware of our selfishness and pride, repenting of our sin, and then asking God to transform us while intentionally seeking to live from a place of self-giving love. What would this process look like in your own life?

CHAPTER 4

Dad Gum Rules

Rules are essential. I don't always like rules, but they are essential. Even some of the rules I thought were dumb as a kid, I now understand as a parent. "Don't run with that in your mouth!" "You're gonna poke your eye out!" "Stop licking that!" My younger self would never have dreamed of saying some of the things that have come out of my mouth as a parent.

I remember one day I was working on something outside on our deck. My son was "helping me" and playing outside as well. We have a water dish on our deck for our "outside/inside" cat. The water dish often sits stagnate and in the humid summer months gets… real nasty. I remember watching helplessly as my son started to bend down and drink the green water like a dog. It was like a slow motion scene from a commercial as I yelled "Noooo….Don't drink that!" I couldn't get up our deck ramp fast enough. I guess he's just boosting his immune system right?

There are things in life that are better for us not to do. Our well-being depends on it sometimes. When I was in college I worked for a home improvement store during the summers.

One of the most fun jobs I have had. I loved driving the fork truck, the order picker lift, and the reach truck (we called it the Star Wars). Actually, I wasn't very good at driving the Star Wars. It had an inverted steering wheel and a joystick that was counterintuitive. I didn't use it enough to become competent at driving it.

The order picker lift is used to raise a person up to stock or to retrieve larger items from the top shelves. The order picker lift has a harness that attaches to a cable on the machine. The harness is a safety measure that protects employees from falling which also protects the company from a lawsuit. There are strict rules that come with earning a license to use these machines. One of the rules is that you have to be harnessed in at all times. Even if you are not up in the air but are just driving it on the ground. You are to be harnessed and hooked in at all times.

I worked on the morning stocking crew for a couple of months one summer so I got to use several different machines quite often. When customers were in the store we always had to block off aisles we were working in and have a "spotter" accompany us. The stocking crew starts before the store opens so we didn't have to follow those particular rules. But, we were still to be harnessed in at all times. I had to be at the store at 4am, so you can imagine that I was drowsy pretty much all of the time. One morning I was putting boxes of our outdoor grills up in top stock. As I was stocking the grills about 15ft in the air, I noticed that I had forgotten to hook the harness to the safety cable!

I immediately hooked my harness in and thanked God that my manager didn't see. I could have likely been fired on the spot! For good reason too. I stocked grills, heavy toilets, and other larger items using that machine. It would not take much for one to lose their balance and fall. The harness and safety cable rules were in place for my own good.

Rules also bring order to chaos. Could you imagine driving on the interstate without any laws and etiquette guidelines? Or, try playing any game or sport without rules. Sports are fun to play, but the rules make the sport possible. For example, I like to play a pickup game of basketball here and there. The basic rules that make a game of basketball possible are agreed upon wherever you go. Even variations in the game like whether we're keeping score by 1s and 2s or 2s and 3s, don't change the fundamental rules about dribbling, defending, and scoring. Without the rules, the game would be chaos.

Rules bring order out of chaos and protection from danger. As a parent, I am a big fan of rules, boundaries, and outlet covers—things that keep my children alive. However, an inordinate focus on rules and boundaries actually becomes life-draining rather than life-giving. Think about the sports analogy. The referees focus on the rules of the game, but they don't play the game. Likewise, the athletes play the game, they don't referee. If your only focus is on the rules, you will never play the game.

Pharisees and Torah

The Scriptures are full of commands from God. Many of them seem confusing because they were given to the nation of Israel. Israel was to live according to God's Laws and be a reflection of God's purpose for humanity to the rest of the nations. To us the Laws in the Old Testament sometimes seem weird and even extreme. For the Israelites, these laws actually looked a lot like other Ancient Near Eastern law codes.

There were unique differences though. For example, a lot of other Ancient Near Eastern cultures valued property more than people so the punishment for stealing was more severe than the punishment for murder. God flips the script on this and says, "No, human life matters more" by prescribing harsher punishments for stealing life.[33] Several of the Laws actually emphasize life in contrast to death in ways that would have made sense to the Israelites. God also gave Israel powerful rituals and symbols for how to worship and relate to him. All these symbols and rituals were meant to help them focus the entirety of their lives on God.

God gave them several rituals and festivals that were meant to be gifts. The Sabbath was meant to instill a weekly rhythm of resting and refocusing on God. God was the source of their identity, not their productivity. God gave them annual festivals, the Sabbatical year, and the year of Jubilee as gifts. These were gifts that were intended to help them facilitate

---

[33] Craig G. Bartholomew and Michael W. Goheen, *The Drama of Scripture: Finding our Place in the Biblical Story* (Grand Rapids: Baker Academic, 2014), 68.

their relationship with God by integrating their ritual worship into the pattern of their lives. They also often involved food and were celebratory. Meaning, they were fun like our holiday traditions.

By the time of Jesus, the Pharisees had turned many of these gifts into rigid rules that had to be followed meticulously. The Pharisees and rabbis had identified 613 commands in the Torah. These 613 commands were dissected, categorized, and expounded upon in the Talmud. The Talmud's exposition on the Law was meant to help faithful Jews to keep the Law as perfectly as humanly possible. The Talmud wasn't necessarily meant to add to the Law per se. It was supposed to clarify the Law by helping people know what exactly it meant to "keep the Sabbath," for example.

For the faithful Israelite, it was extremely important to distinguish and revere the holiness of God. The Israelites believed that they could experience God's presence so long as they upheld the guidelines for ritual purity. If they failed to uphold God's standards, judgment would come upon them. The Israelites knew this all too well. Much of the Old Testament chronicles the downfall of Israel as God removes his hand of protection.

The divided kingdoms, Israel and Judah, fell one after the other into the hands of foreign rulers. The Northern Kingdom of Israel fell to the Assyrian Empire in 722 BC. Nearly 200 years later in 587 BC, the Southern Kingdom of Judah was conquered and the Temple was destroyed by the Babylonian

Empire. The prophets attribute these downfalls to Israel's covenant unfaithfulness.

In 539 BC, under the Persian Empire, a number of Jews were permitted to return to Jerusalem and rebuild the Temple.[34] Many other Jews decided to remain as residents in the foreign lands and became known as the Diaspora. Exile was all they had known, and the land they were in had become home. It is suggested that the origination of the synagogue was during the Exilic Period as the Israelites sought to preserve their cultural and religious heritage. The synagogue became a place of worship, prayer, and the study of the Scriptures since they could not go to the Temple. The synagogue also became a community center where educational, judicial, and political activities took place.[35]

Sometime during the period between the Old Testament and the New Testament it is believed that the sect that would become known as the Pharisees took shape. The Pharisees served as teachers of the oral traditions of the Torah in the synagogues. The Pharisees were "inspired with an urgent sense of the need for two things: (1) revolutionary change in the nation, to separate Israel completely from the ideas and practices of the pagans; and (2) radical obedience to the Torah among God's faithful ones."[36] It is important to note that the

---

[34] Bartholomew and Goheen, *The Drama of Scripture: Finding our Place in the Biblical Story*, 110 and 119.

[35] Bartholomew and Goheen, *The Drama of Scripture: Finding our Place in the Biblical Story*, 120

[36] Bartholomew and Goheen, *The Drama of Scripture: Finding our Place in the Biblical Story*, 132

origination and motivation of the Pharisees was characterized by a sincere desire to obey Yahweh.

The Exile and the formation of the synagogue and the sect of the Pharisees are all important pieces of the New Testament context. Since the fall of Israel and Judah was due to their unfaithfulness, the concern for Covenantal faithfulness manifested in strict Torah observance in matters of ritual purity. Faithful Torah observance was defined by the standards of the Pharisees: "…careful attention to food laws, tithing, Sabbath keeping, and the choice of 'acceptable' mealtime companions— these all are parts of the Pharisees' strategy to keep themselves pure." [37]

Don't miss what has shaped the religious context of Jesus' day. The Pharisees sincerely wanted to obey God and remain faithful to the Covenant. They wanted to teach and lead Israel to do the same. On the surface, this is not a bad thing. The problem? Their focus turned legalistic as they became more consumed with the letter of the law than the heart of the law. Time and time again their confrontations with Jesus had to do with his disregard for their traditions.

The gospel authors could not include every detail about Jesus' life. The gospels are not chronological, play-by-play accounts of Jesus' life. Each gospel author constructs and organizes his gospel account on purpose, including the scenes from Jesus' ministry that emphasize their purpose. Matthew, Mark, and Luke both tell about the time that Jesus called Levi

---

[37] Bartholomew and Goheen, *The Drama of Scripture: Finding our Place in the Biblical Story*, 147.

or Matthew the tax collector to follow him. [38] Apparently, this event made an impact and it is important for understanding Jesus.

Tax collectors were traitors. They collected taxes from their fellow Israelites on behalf of Rome. Not only that, they inflated the taxes people owed so that they could pocket extra for themselves. They were greedy traitors who partnered with the pagan, pig-eating, polytheistic Romans. They were viewed as scum. For the supposed Messiah to call one of *their* kind to follow him was unthinkable. For many observant Jews, the kind of men that Jesus called to be his disciples would have disqualified him from being the *true* Messiah.

After Jesus calls Matthew (Levi's Greek name) to follow him, Matthew honors him by inviting him to his house for dinner. To be a guest in someone's home was a social statement. To be a guest and to share a meal with someone implied mutual acceptance.[39] It was to say, "We belong in relationship together." Jesus was publicly declaring that the boundaries and social constructs that determine whether 'their kind' should associate together didn't apply there.

Matthew also invited all his other shady friends to the meal. Meaning, Jesus wasn't just hanging out with one, recently converted sinner. No. He was eating with *sinners*. Plural. The Pharisees were appalled. How could this man, who presumed

---

[38] Matthew 9:10-17, Mark 2:15-22, Luke 5:29-39

[39] Tremper Longman III and David E. Garland, *Expositor's Bible Commentary: Matthew & Mark* (Grand Rapids: Zondervan, 2007), 125

to have authority to teach other people about God, associate with tax collectors and sinners?

Another time, Jesus went to participate in the service of a local synagogue.[40] There was a man there who had a withered hand. He was likely born with some form of phocomelia. The Pharisees ask Jesus if it is lawful to do the "work" of healing on the Sabbath. They anticipated that he would say "yes," giving them grounds to accuse him.

Jesus calls them out on their hypocrisy. He responds, "If you had a sheep that fell into a well on the Sabbath, wouldn't you work to pull it out? Of course you would. And how much more valuable is a person than a sheep! Yes, the law permits a person to do good on the Sabbath."[41] The Pharisees knew Yahweh valued life, so rescuing a sheep from a well was permissible. This man's deformity was not a life or death issue. Or so they thought.

Valuing life is about more than just valuing that people have oxygen in their lungs. Valuing life means you also value *things that are life-giving*. It means we value restoring and respecting the dignity of people who are created in the image of God. Healing is fundamentally a life-giving endeavor that reflects the God who gives life. To heal is to do good, and only God is good. Therefore, to do good is permissible. For Jesus, there was absolutely no tension between honoring the Sabbath and healing the man. He didn't hesitate for a moment.

---

[40] Matthew 12:9-14

[41] Matthew 12:11-12 (NLT)

The Pharisees were enraged. The irony of their reaction is almost humorous. Matthew tells us that they called a meeting after this incident. The only order of business on the agenda? How to kill Jesus. Their self-righteous legalism and their adherence to religious tradition was so deeply rooted that there was absolutely no conviction that plotting to kill Jesus was wrong. Their legalism blinded them to the point that they were able to justify plotting a murder.

Friend of Sinners

Several years ago, I was in our youth room getting ready for the youth band practice. I helped play guitar in the youth group, and since I cannot sing, the youth pastor's wife worked with our student vocalists. Her day job at the time was working in the admissions department at a Christian college.

In my humble opinion, the college is in no way "liberal" or "progressive." The college is firmly grounded in balanced and conservative doctrinal convictions. I am sure they attract students from all over the doctrinal spectrum. There are some students who disagree with some of their views but love the college, and there are some students who fully align with everything the college affirms.

That evening Alley came in visibly upset. The youth pastor and I could tell that she had been crying. Her husband asked her what was wrong. Alley proceeded to tell us about the phone call she had just received before coming to youth band practice. She receives phone calls from disgruntled parents all the time. Sometimes it is about financial aid. Sometimes it is about a disappointing visit they had. Sometimes it is about the doctrinal errors of the college. This particular phone call had to do with the latter.

A mom called Alley and was furious because her daughter told her that a faculty member had shared a story about their LGBTQ+ friend. That's right. The mom was furious because a faculty member was friends with... a sinner. (Which last time I checked actually included all of us.)

The mom berated Alley over the phone, questioning everything from the college's doctrinal purity to Alley's personal salvation. The mom spewed accusation after accusation at Alley condemning the college and this admissions counselor she barely knew. Alley had to mute the phone so that the mom couldn't hear that she was physically shaking and crying on the other end. Alley had to maintain her composure and stay professional because it is her job, but it wasn't the best part of her day to say the least.

What compels people, who claim to follow Christ, to behave in such a manner? How on earth could this mom believe that her actions were not only ok, but God-honoring? The church is made up of imperfect people. We are going to make mistakes and we are going to hurt others. But, it is one thing to make mistakes, acknowledge those mistakes, and repent of them. It is quite another thing to believe our mistakes are actually holy—to believe Jesus would be ok with our self-righteous, legalistic behaviors.

Sadly, I believe a lot of well-meaning Christians have been deceived into thinking that their self-righteous piety makes them more holy. I say "well-meaning" because I believe a lot of people have been taught to believe God desires our rigid adherence to religious rules. There is no other way that this mom could talk to another human being the way she did to Alley and walk away thinking she did the Lord's work. The irony of the whole story is that there are a number of scenes in the gospels where the religious leaders are raving mad at Jesus for the very same reason this woman was mad—he is friends with sinners.

This is why legalism is so insidious. God's commands aren't something we just throw off as inconsequential. How we live matters. Genuine faith and genuine belief always manifest in outward actions that honor God and obey his commands. Obedience and legalism are not one and the same though. Legalism masks itself as obedience, but is truly concerned with score-keeping. Obedience, on the other hand, is concerned with love.

When the rules become a measuring stick by which we assess our own holiness, then they have become a stumbling block. Not only that, we can't help but start assessing the holiness of other people. Our rule-based assessments of ourselves and other people become value estimates. No longer do people have intrinsic worth because they are created in the image of God. Rather, the worth of other people becomes dependent on their works of obedience. When this happens, someone who identifies as LGBTQ+ is no longer worthy of our friendship.

Not only that, legalism is often based on the traditions of men that are loosely based on God's commands. And, these human traditions are often shaped more by one's cultural context than by God's Word. When our rules are shaped more by our unique and narrow experience of the world than by God's heart, they are certain to be legalistic.

I read a humorous story about a Southern American pastor and wife who traveled to the UK for a ministry opportunity. The local ministry contact that picked up the pastoral couple from the airport was appalled that the pastor's wife kept saying the "F" word. A word that was entirely inappropriate to say in the UK. The word the pastor's wife used so flippantly? "Fanny." That's right. She said "fanny." As in, her bottom. In the UK, it means something else entirely.[42]

Is saying "fanny" sinful since it means something so offensive in the UK? Is it essentially a "cuss word?" I suppose that depends on whether you say it in Alabama or England. Some of our legalistic rules are culturally and contextually bound.

Think about that. Some of the rules we are so adamant about are based on our cultural experiences and not on God's Word. Hugh Halter captures the extent of certain Christian traditions that, in my opinion, are kind of ridiculous:

> While my parents were growing up, they were part of a holiness tradition that had a heightened focus on "not sinning" and, in fact, not getting within 10 miles of the smell of sin. No dice on movies, no dice at all for that matter. No art, bowling, alcohol, tobacco use of any kind, no dancing, no playing

---

[42] I don't recommend looking it up.

cards, no drums in church, no saying "Darn" because that's a derivative of *dang*, and *dang* is a Latin ancestor or third cousin to damn. Same with *shoot*, *shucks*, *crap*, *geez*, and *cripes*. I'm not sure where they found some loopholes, but my uncle could say, "Dad gum," and all my parents and relatives played the card game Rook. I think they told me once that the Raven on the top of the Rook box is a Greek expression of the dove or Holy Spirit bird. I bought it at the time, but not anymore. After all these years, I finally found out that Rook was okay because it has no face cards. You know, no king other than God, no queen, as she's a seductress, and that poor suicidal Jack was too emotionally unstable to look at.[43]

While these rigid rules are somewhat humorous, they are not innocent. Legalism reduces our covenant-bound, love founded relationship with God to a subjective checklist determined by human traditions.

Remember, legalism is the problem not obedience. I want my son to obey me. More than that though, I want him to know that I love him. I want him to know that my love and his value are never dependent on his obedience. But, because I love him, my commands come from a place of love. I want what is best for him. I want him to trust in my love. Notice that. I

---

[43] Hugh Halter and Matt Smay, *The Tangible Kingdom: Creating Incarnational Community* (Hoboken: Jossey-Bass, 2008), 135.

don't want him to trust in my commands. *I want him to trust in my love, and therefore trust that the commands come from a place of love.* I also want him to obey me because he loves me. I want his love more than I want his legalistic adherence to rules.

Similarly, I love my wife. Because I love her, there are boundaries that are in place to protect the intimacy of our relationship. One of the boundaries is that neither of us hang out with someone of the opposite sex one-on-one just for fun on the regular. Neither of us cultivate one-on-one friendships with people of the opposite sex. We have friends of the opposite sex, but we are each other's best friend.

Our relationship isn't characterized by rigid adherence to a list of rules. Our relationship is not focused on rules at all. Our relationship is focused on loving one another well, and loving one another well means we do and don't do certain things. Loving one another well means that we strive to practice behaviors and attitudes that cultivate love between us. Again, this means there are "rules" in a sense, but the focus is not on the rules. The focus is on loving the other.

A husband can focus on not cheating on his wife, and not love his wife. There are a number of marriages in which the partners are physically faithful, but not intimately connected. A husband who focuses on loving his wife will not then cheat on her. This order is significant. Love gives way to faithful obedience, but faithful obedience does not necessarily equal love.

Love Not Law

God wants your love. He wants your obedience for sure. But, he wants obedience that is provoked by a deep awareness of his great love. He wants obedience that is inspired and motivated by love. He wants our obedience to be our love response. A response that is more concerned with loving God and others well than with adhering to a list of rules. Rules aren't the problem. In fact, they can be life-saving and chaos-reducing. The problem is when we are obsessed with rigid adherence to the rules. Rules become a problem when our obsession is fed by our belief that our value depends on it. Rules are a problem when other people's value depends on their performance too. When this happens, we will certainly miss the heart of Christ, and more likely embrace the heart of a Pharisee.

Reflection/Discussion Questions

1. Why are rules important? How are they sometimes necessary?

2. How would you describe your natural disposition? Are you inclined to rigidly follow rules or are you convinced rules are meant to be broken?

3. What is the difference between being observant of important "rules" and becoming legalistic?

4. In what ways does legalism miss the point of God's laws?

5. Anthony suggested that faithful obedience will flow from our pursuit of loving God, but faithful obedience will not necessarily produce love for God. Do you agree or disagree? Why or why not?

CHAPTER 5

Restaurant Servers, Sinners, and Stones

One of the things I don't see a lot of these days is grace. People lambaste those they disagree with on social media, individuals often assume the worst of motives in their coworker's errors, and many customers are often ruthlessly ungracious with their waiter or waitress. These might be silly examples, but they are small examples of our general lack of grace for others.

One afternoon I was eating with some friends at a local Thai restaurant. The crab cheese Rangoons are the perfect combination of sweet and savory and deep fried goodness. The chicken Panang curry is fantastic—but spicy! It is not a franchise or a big operation. Most times there is only one server working. The service isn't extremely fast, but I also wouldn't say it is slow. My food has always come out hot and fresh. I have generally had a good experience at this local joint.

That afternoon, there was a guy who was sitting at the table parallel to ours. I am not sure what all was wrong with his order, but he made a big stink about it. I think he was upset by how slow his food came out, but whatever his problem, I just remember feeling embarrassed for that man. He ripped the server up and down for what seemed like a minor issue that mostly had to do with his lack of patience rather than her failure to provide hospitable service.

The poor server working the floor that day was visibly distraught and overly apologetic. When we went to check out, we could tell she was emotionally upset. Her value as a human being had been publicly degraded. With no regard for who she was as a person, the man humiliated her. My friends and I left her a big tip because all of us were appalled at the man's ungracious display and we wanted to attempt to lift her spirits.

What is it about our attitudes towards other people that can sometimes be viciously ungracious? I have worked in customer service. People can be downright mean. People are often extremely ungracious towards their neighbor, but adamant that they themselves deserve grace. We want people to give us the benefit of the doubt. We want people to take into consideration the sort of day we have had that led up to our faux pas. We want people to be understanding of us. Yet, we are so often unrelenting in our established expectations of other people.

I think part of this tendency is the reality that we know when someone has wronged us. Whether we like churchy words like "sin" or "trespass" or not, we know that there is such a thing as injustice and evil. We are particularly aware of this reality when someone trespasses against us. We know there is a right, moral, good, or loving way to treat other people.

Conversely, we know there are inappropriate, immoral, and unjust ways of treating other people.

These wrongs need to be made right. However, a wrong cannot be undone. Sometimes a wrong can be balanced or paid for. We used to host a small group in our home every other week. We had a group of young couples and young parents that attended. One evening, one of the other couple's kid hit our flat-screen TV with something and damaged the LCD screen. The mom had just shared about some health insurance issues they were dealing with that were unfair and stressful. We really like our TV, but we really didn't feel right about asking them to pay for it. We figured we would try to find a Black Friday deal the next week and just eat the cost. The other family wasn't having it. They insisted on paying for the TV and forced us to take an envelope of cash.

We could have done the awkward back and forth argument for days, but we decided to just accept the money. My wife said that some people really have a hard time not paying for the damage. She wanted our friends to not be weird around us or feel like there was a debt hanging over our relationship. Their paying for it was a way of absolving the guilt associated with the damaged TV. The act could not be undone, but it has been paid for. There is nothing hanging over our friendship.

However, there are some wrongs that can't be paid for. There are some acts that no dollar amount can remedy. I know of a couple of accidents that have happened in our area that took the lives of young people. The person at fault can never pay for the consequences of their error. They can never replace the life a parent lost. When it comes to the accumulated mass of our own sins that have contributed to the brokenness in this world, we cannot pay enough to balance the scales. We're bankrupt before God.

We know this and we are thankful for God's grace found in Jesus. When we're the perpetrator, we want to experience grace infused forgiveness. The problem is that we are not always as quick to extend the same grace we've received to others. When we're the victim, we want our pound of flesh.

The problem is that the score is never truly settled. The gospel calls us to recognize this. On the cross, the sinless One identified with sinners and victims. He was the victim of a mock trial and suffered one of the most inhumane executions that humanity has conjured up. He suffered injustice while also dying as a criminal and in so doing he identified with humanity's sin. He absorbed sin and injustice by nailing it to the cross.

The cross is God's definitive answer to injustice and sin. He will not stand idly by while people are oppressed and wronged. Yet, he will also not hold humanity's sins against them should they give up all of their efforts of saving themselves and truly abandon themselves to the grace of God. Paul says it like this, "All this is from God, who reconciled us to himself through Christ and gave us the ministry of reconciliation: that God was reconciling the world to himself in Christ, not counting people's sins against them."[44]

---

[44] 2 Corinthians 5:18-19

This is good news because we are both victim and perpe-trator. We need both justice and grace. When we realize that we are just as guilty as anyone else, we have to abandon our old ways of evaluating other people. We have to admit that we are all on a level playing field, meaning God's grace for us is also for *them*.

Pardon Me

Have you ever had your kid walk in on you and your spouse while you were in the middle of some quality time (wink, wink)? Nothing disrupts the mood like your toddler barging in asking for cereal. John writes about an awkward incident in his gospel where a woman was caught in the act of adultery, or at least that is what she was accused of being caught doing.[45]

Here's the scene: Jesus is teaching in the temple courts—this is a very public and open area. Think of it as an open court-yard in a public park or like the common area in a shopping mall. People would gather around to listen to rabbis publicly teaching. As people gathered to listen to the Master Teacher, a group of scribes and Pharisees disrupt the gathering, bringing the promiscuous woman to Jesus. In front of everyone gath-ered, they make their accusations.

> "Teacher, this woman has been caught in the act of
> adultery. Now in the Law Moses commanded us
> to stone such women. So what do you say?"

---

[45] John 8:1-11 (ESV)

83

Being under the jurisdiction of Rome, the Jewish people could not carry out executions without Rome's approval. If Jesus said to stone her, he would be going against Rome's law. If he said not to stone her, he would be going against the Law of Moses. At least, that was how they were looking at it for their intention was to trap Jesus. They wanted to find a reason to condemn him. They weren't picky either. If they couldn't condemn him based on the Law of Moses, maybe they could catch him saying something against Rome so that they could go tattle on him to them.

Jesus rarely played their games by their rules in the gospel accounts. Jesus bent down and began doodling in the sand. That's right. Jesus started drawing, writing, or scribbling with his finger in the dirt. What he wrote or drew, no one knows. Some have suggested that he was writing the specific sins that the religious leaders standing there had committed. Others have suggested that he is writing out the Old Testament laws concerning adultery. The Law states that the man *and* the woman are to be punished if caught in adultery.[46] The scribes and Pharisees only brought the woman. It takes two to tango. They themselves were breaking the Law.

Frustrated by his art work in the sand, the religious leaders continued to press him on the matter. Jesus stands up and says, "Let him who is without sin among you be the first to throw a stone at her." Notice what Jesus did not say. He did not say, "Whoever has not sinned as badly, or whoever's sin is not as public, perverted, or offensive...go ahead and throw

---

[46] Leviticus 20:10

the first stone at her." No, he says, "Let him who is *without* sin…" Any sin.

One by one they walk away. Until it was only Jesus and the woman there in the temple court. Jesus says to the woman, "Woman, where are they? Has no one condemned you?"

She replied, "No one, Lord."

Jesus' next response is mind-boggling. Remember, Jesus is God in the flesh. The one who is sinless and has every right to throw stones. The one who this woman has ultimately sinned against for our sins ultimately defy God. Jesus says to this woman, "*Neither do I condemn you*; go, and from now on sin no more."

When grace encounters sin, it does not condemn… it scandalously pardons. Grace does not condone sin, but it does freely forgive. We get hung up here because we think to pardon is to also make allowance for sin. People get concerned that if we emphasize grace too much people will believe it is a license to sin. We have to balance our grace out with just enough hellfire and brimstone so people don't get the wrong idea about this God the Father guy.

Jesus shows us what the heart of the Father is like. Jesus demonstrates that his grace is sufficient. Grace is sufficient for sin—even sexual sin, or whatever sin we tend to write off as unforgivable. Paul understood this. As a former Pharisee who was very familiar with the Law, his shift from ritual observance to relational intimacy is astounding. He went from working to earn God's favor to working to convince people that the favor of God was already available to them through Christ. To the church at Rome Paul wrote,

> Now the law came in to increase the trespass, but where sin increased, grace abounded all the more, so that, as sin reigned in death, grace also might reign through righteousness leading to eternal life through Jesus Christ our Lord. [47]

Paul is saying that the Law revealed sin to us. Sin was already present, but the Law named it, made us aware, and the more aware of sin we are, the more sin there seems to be. But what Paul writes next is profoundly counterintuitive: "...where sin increased, grace abounded all the more."

The language Paul uses here is extravagant. He is ecstatic as he explains that God's grace is as inexhaustible as his love. It is as infinite as his nature. It is as limitless as his power. Where sin appears to have exceeded any reasonable measure of pardoning grace, grace outdoes it. Grace exhausts sin's power.

In other words, there is no sin—no matter how grotesque, selfish, malicious, or perverse—that can compare to the fathomless grace of God. There is no prodigal who has wandered too far. There is no skeptic whose doubts are too big for the transforming power of God's grace. There is no heart so hard that God can't transform it. The invitation of the gospel is to believe this both for ourselves and for others. To believe that

---

[47] Romans 5:20 (ESV)

God's grace is sufficient for our salvation and that it is sufficient for covering the wrongs of others too.

Grace is arguably the most ridiculous and irrational concept in the world. The Sunday school understanding of God's grace is that "grace is unmerited favor." This is too rehearsed and we don't realize the meaning of "unmerited." Grace is the complete forgiveness of a debt. Grace is my student loans being paid for by someone else with no strings attached.

We ponder that and go, "Oh, I see," but we forget that this is one of those things we never believe would happen. I cannot comprehend that someone would pay for my debt without at least asking a favor of me. This is one of those completely hypothetical scenarios that we claim to understand, but in practice, we have a really hard time actually living it out. It is one those "too good to be true" sort of realities.

Grace is the parent of a murdered child embracing the drunk driver that caused their child's death. Grace is the victim of rape hoping for the redemption of the twisted soul that committed the act. Grace is the child who offers forgiveness to their abusive father. Grace is a spouse loving the other in spite of unfaithfulness and making the way for restoration. Grace is ridiculous. Grace is unscientific. Grace does not work in the favor of the one who imparts it.

Grace is God Almighty surrendering divine attributes in order to truly know the human experience and then offering his life to pay the debt of our rebellion. Grace is God paying for hatred, anger, violence, genocide, abortion, murder, lust, greed, injustice, poverty, selfishness, envy, adultery, dishonesty, rebellion, brokenness—grace is God taking *my* place for my sin, for my broken and depraved heart.

Where sin abounds, grace is more.

Stone Dropping

I heard a pastor preach on the John 8 passage and in his sermon he challenged his congregation to be "a stone-dropping church."[48] I like that. We are so quick to throw stones at other people. The more legalistic we are the quicker we are to throw stones. The more self-righteous we are the quicker we are to throw stones. If you are quick to throw stones at other people, that might be an indicator that something is not quite right in your heart.

Stone-throwing at others looks like being quick to assume the motives of people's actions. Stone-throwing looks like having a hierarchy of sins by which you stack people up against to determine the authenticity of their faith. If they don't measure up you cast them out and determine that they are either "weak Christians" or "inauthentic Christians."

Throwing stones at other people's sins usually means we have an inaccurate view of your own sins. It usually means we fair better on the balancing scales than others. At least, when we are evaluated according to *the* hierarchy of sins *we* have constructed.

When we have categorized other people's sins as being worse than our own sin, we legitimize our stone-throwing.

---

[48] I remember the sermon was by Judah Smith

Paul said that he was the worst of sinner's. [49] I think this is the only way to accurately see ourselves. When we come to realize that the same grace that saved us is the same sufficient grace that can save *those people*, the orientation of our heart is transformed from desiring to throw stones to desiring the restoration of others.

That hierarchy of sins list often has a self-destructive side to it too. When our sins aren't on the list, we simply judge and throw stones at others. But, when we mess things up and find ourselves struggling with something on that list...well, then we start throwing stones at ourselves.

When we start struggling with addiction, when our marriage falls apart, when our kids wander from the faith, when we start responding to life's trials in unhealthy ways—well, the tables are turned and we turn on ourselves. We start allowing the lies of the enemy to define us. We start believing that we are too far from the reach of grace for God to save us.

Self-directed stone-throwing is just as harmful to the gospel of grace as others-directed stone-throwing. The gospel is that you can't and that's ok because he already did. Believing this new identity is the mysterious way to victory. Believing God's grace has triumphed breaks the back of Satan's lies and therefore looses the bonds of sin. Shame thrives in an environment of non-grace. Shame is the devil's game. Grace chases out shame and makes room for wholeness. Wholeness is the way to holiness.

---

[49] 1 Timothy 1:15

Whether you are prone to throwing stones at others or yourself, maybe it is time to drop the stones. Maybe it is time to live *in* grace, *by* grace, while *extending* grace. Maybe it is time to see other people as children in bondage needing liberated rather than enemies needing to be eliminated. Maybe it is time to remember that if not for God, their situation could be yours. Grace makes the way for so many other crucial shifts that must take place in our hearts if we are going to look like Jesus.

Return Fire

On September 6, 2018, an off-duty Dallas police officer made a horrific mistake. Amber Guyger entered the apartment of Botham Jean where she shot and killed him. She claimed that she thought she was going into her own apartment. Jean's apartment was directly beneath hers and the apartment complex has nearly identical floor plans. She claimed that the door was ajar and when she entered there was a man inside the dark apartment. Believing him to be an intruder, she shot and killed him.

The incident garnered a lot of media attention because Amber was a white, female police officer and Botham was an unarmed Black man sitting in the living room of his own apartment. Whether Amber's claims are genuine or not, the fact is that she didn't follow protocol. If she was truly concerned that there was an intruder in the apartment, she should have called for backup. The fact is that she went to the wrong floor and entered the wrong apartment. A tragically, accidental mistake maybe, but one that was completely her fault.

The trial and sentencing stirred up several controversies because for many Black Americans it was another example of police brutality overlooked. Amber received a fairly lenient sentencing. Adding to the media coverage was the statement from Brandt Jean, Botham's younger brother. Brandt Jean extended a peculiar and unusual degree of grace and forgiveness to Amber Guyger during his victim impact statement. Here's the transcript of his statement:

> If you truly are sorry, I know I can speak for myself, I forgive you. And I know if you go to God and ask him, he will forgive you.
>
> And I don't think anyone can say it — again I'm speaking for myself and not on behalf of my family — but I love you just like anyone else.
>
> And I'm not going to say I hope you rot and die, just like my brother did, but I personally want the best for you. And I wasn't going to ever say this in front of my family or anyone, but I don't even want you to go to jail. I want the best for you, because I know that's exactly what Botham would want you to do.
>
> And the best would be: give your life to Christ.

> I'm not going to say anything else. I think giving your life to Christ would be the best thing that Botham would want you to do.
>
> Again, I love you as a person. And I don't wish anything bad on you.
>
> I don't know if this is possible, but can I give her a hug, please? Please?[50]

Some people disapproved of the judge's decision, but the judge granted his request. He allowed Brandt Jean to hug Amber Guyger. The video footage is quite moving as Amber sobs in his arms while asking for forgiveness.

Brandt's statement provoked a wide spectrum of responses. Some shared the video footage on social media platforms and heralded it as an outstanding example of Christ-like forgiveness. Others warned people that, while his forgiveness was Christ-like and admirable, it should not erase the racial implications of the incident. Black people have been asked to overlook, forgive, tolerate, and endure white oppression for centuries. Some felt that this was just another example of injustice.

I am a white male who has lived a fairly middle-class lifestyle my whole life. I have also lived in regions of the Midwest that are fairly homogenous. I have made incredibly ignorant

---

[50] "Brandt Jean to Amber Guyger: 'I Forgive You, I Love You, Give Your Life to Christ'." *National Catholic Register*, www.ncregister.com/blog/pjsmith/botham-jeans-brother-to-amber-guyer-i-forgive-you-i-love-you-give-your-life.

statements about racial issues at several points in my life. I am trying to grow in my awareness of my ignorance. I try to listen better. I try to understand more. I do not want to downplay the racial issues interwoven in this story. However, I would still find this level of forgiveness and grace to be beautiful regardless of the victim's ethnicity.[51]

Similar stories that do not have the racial implications still move me to see the beauty of grace and forgiveness. In October 2006, Charles Roberts IV entered an Amish schoolhouse in Nickel Mines, PA, where he shot ten school girls killing five of them and then committed suicide afterward. In the wake of the shooting, the Amish community gathered and demonstrated an unusual amount of forgiveness going so far as to visit with Robert's widow, parents, and in-laws. Their act of forgiveness went against the typical response of grieving victims.

Why am I sharing about examples of forgiveness in a chapter about grace? It may seem out of place, especially considering the reality that I have another chapter on forgiveness, but the reason is because grace and forgiveness go hand in

---

[51] I believe it is important to note right here that part of the issue is that many Black Americans feel that Black people have had to forgive the trespasses of white people regardless of white people's concession of guilt or remorse. This wound is further inflicted when white people claim no need to confess or repent of the sins of their ancestors by simply saying that "I didn't own slaves" or "I am not racist." There is actually biblical precedent for collective confession and repentance even for sins you were not a part of committing. Daniel is one example. He repents of the sins of *his people and identifies with their guilt* (Daniel 9:1-19). (See also Leviticus 26:40)

hand. Every act of forgiveness is infused with grace. Every act of grace inspires forgiveness. Grace enables forgiveness.

When the Christ-follower returns fire, it should reflect the way of the cross. The way that is characterized by grace and forgiveness. This is a profoundly counterintuitive way of living and viewing people and responding to wrongs. I think this is what Jesus meant when he talked about picking up our cross to follow him or when he said that the way to find ourselves is by losing.[52]

Showing grace to other people makes losers out of us. At least according to the world's standards. It is very un-American, but I would argue that it has the power to change the world. Brennan Manning wrote so beautifully and eloquently about grace. He held the conviction that God really loves those who don't deserve it. This conviction was birthed out of his own experience of God's love for him. He was a prodigal son who was overwhelmed by the reception of the Father. He focused his life's work on sharing this grace with others. He wrote,

> My message, unchanged for more than fifty years, is this: God loves you unconditionally, as you are and not as you should be because nobody is as they should be. It is the message of grace...A grace that pays the eager beaver who works all day long the same wages as the grinning drunk who shows up at ten till five...A grace that hikes up the robe and runs breakneck toward the prodigal reeking of sin

---

[52] Matthew 16:25

and wraps him up and decides to throw a party no ifs, ands, or buts…This grace is indiscriminate compassion. It works without asking anything of us…Grace is sufficient even though we huff and puff with all our might to try to find something or someone it cannot cover. Grace is enough…Jesus is enough.[53]

When you come to really believe that grace is sufficient, it opens a whole new world of possibilities. It opens up the possibility that you can be radically made new. It opens up the audacious hope that no one is too far from the reach of God's grace. This hope inspires radical love, compassion, and forgiveness for other people—which defies the power of sin and grave. God's grace calls us to embrace grace. When we embrace grace, we will be compelled to extend grace.

---

[53] Brennan Manning and John Blasé, *All is Grace: A Ragamuffin Memoir* (Colorado Springs: David C Cook, 2011), 192-194.

Reflection/Discussion Questions

1. How does the cross reconcile those things that can't be undone? How Does God make it right? What does it mean that the cross is God's answer to sin—even sins committed against us?

2. In what ways are we sometimes stone throwers instead of stone droppers? Are there categories of sin you find it easy to throw stones at?

3. How does grace both call us and empower us to be stone droppers? Are there any stones aimed at yourself that you need to drop in order to embrace grace?

4. What is the relationship between grace and forgiveness?

5. Anthony stated that, "Showing grace to other people makes losers out of us." Do you agree or disagree? Explain?

CHAPTER 6

Sometimes I Want Revenge

O ne of my favorite movies is *Gladiator* starring Russell Crowe. The movie tells the story of Maximus Decimus Meridius—"The general who became a slave. The slave who became a gladiator. The gladiator who defied an emperor." The movie opens with General Maximus leading the Roman army to victory in an epic battle against the Germanic barbarians. As Emperor Marcus Aurelius congratulates a blood-splattered and war tired Maximus on his victory, the soldiers salute their allegiance. To which Maximus states, "They honor you, Caesar."

"No Maximus. It *is you they honor*." Maximus lifts his sword in response and the legions of soldiers raise a glorious shout of victory. From the opening scene, you come to realize that Maximus is a respected and beloved leader.

Maximus' character is immediately contrasted with the Emperor's son, Commodus. Commodus has been summoned to come to the war front because the aging Marcus Aurelius is planning to name his successor. Commodus is overly confident that his father is going to name him Caesar. A title and position of power that Commodus, as the Emperor's son, has likely dreamed about for his entire life. When his father instead informs him that he is going to name Maximus as his successor, a devastated Commodus smothers his aging father to death.

The next morning the camp is mourning the loss of the Emperor who appears "to have died in his sleep" before officially naming Maximus as Caesar. Maximus is immediately suspicious of foul play and refuses to pledge his allegiance to Commodus. Consequently, Maximus is arrested for treason and informed that his wife and son would be killed as well. Maximus skillfully dodges the sword of his executioner and kills his captors. He mounts a horse and races across Europe in an attempt to get to his family before the Roman Praetorians sent to kill them do.

In spite of his effort, Maximus is too late. You are absorbed into his grief as you see the feet of his lifeless wife and son hanging in the doorway of his home. Consumed with grief and exhausted from his journey, Maximus collapses there on his homestead with little desire to live. He is picked up by nomadic slave traders and sold to Proximo, the owner and beneficiary of a gladiator school.

Maximus, despairing of life itself, has no intention of fighting until he realizes that the gladiator games could take him to Rome. As the epic unfolds, Maximus is driven by a desire for revenge. He desires nothing more than to avenge his family. His experience as a trained soldier lends him to skillfully dominating every fight he is assigned. He soon becomes a fan favorite and after each fight he wins, the crowd erupts as they chant "Spaniard, Spaniard, Spaniard!"

The fights eventually do take Maximus to the Roman Coliseum. The cinematic portrayal of Rome is breathtaking. The Coliseum captivates you as you take in the grandness of its architecture. The first battle in the Coliseum has the feel of a modern football game. The house is packed as the "mob" of Rome has gathered to satisfy their bloodlust. The fight is supposed to be a recreation of the Battle of Carthage and Proximo's slaves are assigned the role of the losers. Maximus uses his military knowledge to strategically defeat the opposing gladiators, much to the delight of the crowd.

Commodus is so impressed that he descends to the Coliseum floor to congratulate and meet the gladiators who "re-wrote" the story. Commodus asks for Maximus to remove his helmet and declare his name. Maximus responds, "My name is Gladiator," and proceeds to turn his back on the emperor.

"How dare you show your back to me! Slave, you will remove your helmet and tell me your name."

Maximus slowly turns, takes his helmet off, and responds, "My name is Maximus Decimus Meridius, commander of the Armies of the North, General of the Felix Legions and loyal servant to the *true* emperor, Marcus Aurelius. Father to a murdered son, husband to a murdered wife. *And I will have my vengeance, in this life or the next.*"

Revenge Sounds So Heroic

That scene is one of the most epic declarations in cinematic history of a hero's resolve to take justice into his own hands. It is a classic "man-movie." Several of my favorite movies portray a character who takes matters into his own hands to assert justice by whatever means necessary: *Taken, The Patriot,* and *Equalizer* are just a couple other movies I really enjoy.

Batman is my favorite super-hero-vigilante. Batman's entire character is built on his quest to exact justice on those who would do harm to other people. His sense of justice is born out of the loss of his parents to a senseless and petty crime. His means of executing justice? Violence. His motivation? Revenge.

While something in me enjoys watching these "heroes" exact justice on evildoers, something else in me knows their violent revenge doesn't undo the brokenness unleashed by their enemies. Sometimes the "hero" saves the day, which some would argue outweighs their questionable methods, but, I also have this question deep down as to whether what they have done in the name of justice is right. Is their rage truly heroic? Is the way they take the life of another human being something we can sincerely and unequivocally declare as "good"? Should we take justice into our own hands? If so, what should it look like?

Road Rage

Every now and then someone will do something so idiotic and reckless on the interstate that it makes my blood boil. Now, you probably do not know me, so you need to know that I am not typically a hot-tempered person. However, I have been so aggravated by the audacious lack of consideration for other people that I have felt justified in my anger. Their recklessness could cost the lives of other people for crying out loud! If my babies are in the car with me, that only ignites my righteous anger all the more.

Sometimes I wish to myself that they would get pulled over. How satisfying would it be to watch someone carelessly zip past you only to see them pulled over a couple miles ahead? It would feel like sweet vindication wouldn't it?

Obviously, if someone is being reckless and almost causing an accident it seems pretty reasonable to be angry. But, I have to confess that sometimes people have just cut me off rudely, but not necessarily dangerously. Their action wouldn't have caused an accident. It just wasn't nice. Exaggerating the magnitude of their carelessness adds to the sense of justification though. Maybe you have never done that, but I have often found myself turning a "molehill into a mountain." My outrage at people's driving blunders is most times disproportionate to the wrong.

One time I actually stopped and asked myself, "Why does this anger me so much? Why does someone cutting me off come across as an affront to my very existence?" I realized, at least for me, it bothers me that someone could deem me worth so little acknowledgment that they could assert their value over mine by cutting me off. I know that sounds deep, but that's what it is really about when we get offended by someone else's inconsideration. They've made a statement about our value, our worth. When someone is rude or inconsiderate of us, it threatens our value by their asserting their value as more important.

Hence, it would seem that our anger at the injustice done to us is really about our identity. We feel wronged when our value has been diminished, disregarded, or discounted. We feel wronged when someone asserts their worth over ours, when someone robs us of value to enhance their own, or when someone simply has little regard for our personhood.

We feel wronged. Sometimes we are justified in our feeling of injustice. Other times, it is really not that big of a deal, but we are so deficient in our own self-worth that we grasp at anything to prop up our identity.

It is in this environment that revenge flourishes because revenge promises to balance the scales. Revenge promises that our value can be restored if we simply take back what is ours. We resort to all sorts of petty actions in our attempt to execute justice. We will gossip about co-workers, undermine our superiors, passive-aggressively jab at our spouses, manipulate our kids, sabotage our peers, write angry posts on social media, brawl, lie, steal, cheat—we will do whatever we deem necessary in order to dominate others so that our value is in fact proven to be worth more than theirs.

See, we don't want justice if it means our enemies are weighed on the same scale as us. Which is why we have such a hard time trusting God to take care of it. We actually want to come out on top. We want retribution; we want justice *and* compensation for being wronged. Therefore, it is obvious that *we must take matters into our own hands.*

Just-is-n't Fair

You know how I said I get mad on the road when people do something rude or stupid? Have you ever been angered by someone's driving mistake only to do something stupid yourself? I have.

I remember one sunny morning I was on my way into the office. Sometimes I would take different routes just to switch up my commute. Do you ever do that? I was taking some roads in the downtown area of our town. For whatever reason, all little towns seem to have some areas where there are these odd one-way streets. As I was zig-zagging through our downtown streets, I came up to an intersection where a one-way intersected with the two-way street I was on. I had a stop sign. The one-way street did not.

Sometimes, I don't really know what goes through my head when I make absent minded mistakes. I likely rolled through my stop sign, assuming the one-way also had a stop sign. Just as I was about to pull through the intersection an SUV passed in front of me. I slammed on my breaks in time, but not before I scared her so badly that she also slammed on her breaks. She had a travel mug of coffee in her hand. You can probably guess how that turned out. She spilled some of her coffee. I made the mistake of making eye contact and I saw her mouth a profanity. I mouthed, "I'm sorry..."

That is just one incident of my own driving mishap. I have driven down a one-way the wrong way, accidentally blown through a stop sign, almost backed into someone—you name it, I've probably made the mistake. When I originally started this chapter none of my driving mistakes had resulted in an at-fault accident with the exception of my very first accident as a teenager. However, recently I rear-ended someone because I looked at my phone for a brief millisecond. Every time I make a driving blunder I feel like an idiot. I am so embarrassed by my absentmindedness. I feel even more foolish many times because earlier in the week I had so little grace with someone else's driving error.

This is exactly why we cannot sit in the judge's seat. Because, "in the same way you judge others, you will be judged, and with the measure you use, it will be measured to you."[54] If my own driving blunders were judged by the standard I judge others, then my license would likely be revoked. We are all terribly guilty of this all of the time. We are biased and we see things from our own vantage point. We *always see our side of the story as more right than other's*. We always sympathize with our own "legitimizing" excuses while leaving others little to no room for excuse.

We judge our co-workers for being lazy and late to work, but when we are late we have reasonable excuses. The kids were difficult, traffic was bad, there was a train again, the battery in the car died because of the winter temperatures, and so on. I remember judging the parenting tactics of other parents *before* I had kids. That was a mistake. If you are married, you have likely used different standards of justice with your spouse. I know I have. I have been quick to call out my wife when she is a little "grumpy," giving her little grace for her

---

[54] Matthew 7:2

snarky attitude. When the tables are turned though, I have legitimizing excuses: I am under a lot of stress at work, the kids were pushing my buttons, I didn't get enough sleep—you get the idea.

I have found it most puzzling and almost humorous the hypocrisy I have seen in the wake of our tense political climate. I am not intending to express a specific political position on any particular topic, but I want to use a brief example I have witnessed. I have personally heard people complain about getting a speeding ticket and about the injustice of taxes. When the law demands consequences to be dealt out to them, they claim "injustice"! Yet, it is often these same people who elevate the American immigration laws to the place of biblical authority declaring, "We must obey the laws of the land." When consequences are applied to someone else, it is not grace or injustice they appeal to. Rather, they demand the letter of the law be met.

We can never be judge and jury. We will always see our own errors as deserving of grace and others as deserving of punishment. It is completely and utterly impossible for us to hold a neutral position. Therefore, our every attempt to balance the scales in any sort of retributive or vengeful way adds to the injustice in our world that must be made right. Think about that. Our revenge efforts add to the chaos of injustice. And, in that way, we are no better off than our enemies.

Jonah and the Fish

Jonah was a prophet during the reign of King Jeroboam II of Israel. Jeroboam II, from a worldly and human perspective, was a successful king. Under his rule, Israel extended her borders and reclaimed territories that were originally part of David and Solomon's Kingdom. Although Israel flourished, Jeroboam II did evil in God's eyes by embracing idolatry and showing disregard for God's Law.

The word of the LORD came to Jonah and called him to go to Nineveh, the capital city of Assyria, to preach a message of coming judgment because of their evil.[55] Embedded in the message of judgment was the call to repentance. Assyria had been a dominant world power in the Middle East, but it is believed that during the time of Jonah there was some political unrest. However, just a century earlier, Israel along with a number of other nations were subject to Assyria.

Assyria was also known for her brutality—prisoners of war were stabbed, impaled, beheaded, flayed alive—you get the picture. Assyria was a terrifying and hated enemy among those conquered and yet to be conquered. Jonah's call to go to Nineveh, an Assyrian city, was not a preferred assignment.

I can't overstate enough all the reasons going to Nineveh was not ideal for Jonah. Jonah, being an Israelite, likely reveled in Assyria's current political instability. Jonah likely hated Assyrians—as in, he hated anyone whose nationality was derived from that people group. Assyria would have been like Nazi Germany if you were to make a more modern comparison. Growing up, we were taught in Sunday school that Jonah was scared of Assyria's cruelty. That might be partially true,

---

[55] Jonah 1:1

but a more accurate understanding of Jonah's position would be to understand this: Jonah was a racist.

Jonah also knew God's heart. Why would someone who hates a particular people group not actually enjoy proclaiming a message of judgment and destruction? Jonah confesses why: "I tried to forestall by fleeing to Tarshish. I knew that you are a *gracious* and *compassionate* God, slow to anger and abounding in love, a God who relents from sending calamity." Jonah knew God is gracious and compassionate.

For reasons of self-preservation and nationalistic prejudice, Jonah decided to deliberately run away from his calling. He boards a ship at Joppa heading for Tarshish. While the exact location of Tarshish is unknown, the port at Joppa along the Mediterranean is the opposite direction of Nineveh.

While aboard the ship, a severe God-sent storm develops threatening the structure of the boat.[56] In the midst of the storm, each sailor calls to his own god, except for Jonah. Jonah is asleep below deck. Appalled, the captain wakes Jonah and urges him to plead for mercy from his god—surely one of the sailors will find favor with his god!

The sailors cast lots in order to either 1.) decide the order of confession or 2.) to determine by fate who is at fault and which deity is offended. When the lot falls on Jonah, Jonah confesses that he is running from Yahweh, the creator of heaven and earth. Jonah tells the crew to throw him overboard. Which is an odd command to obey if you're the rest of the crew, but they went ahead and threw him overboard.

---

[56] Jonah 1:4

Immediately after Jonah is thrown overboard the storm subsides. God sends a large fish (this is important for you to know—it will make your Bible nerd friends proud if you say fish and not whale because the text says "large fish" not whale) that swallows Jonah. As Jonah is inside the belly of this large fish, he prays a prayer of thanksgiving and deliverance. The problem is that "…songs of thanksgiving generally work on the presumption of innocence."[57] Jonah's heart still presumes his justification. Notice his viewpoint: *he* is deserving of deliverance, but he remains insistent that *Assyria* is not.

The fish vomits him out on dry land which is likely analogous to how God feels about his prayer and "apology." Jonah's prayer is kind of like a "sorry, not sorry" prayer. After being vomited onto dry land, God again tells him to go preach to Nineveh. This time he obeys, but according to the text, he puts in the least amount of effort he can while still technically obeying. For example, the recorded message Jonah preaches is incredibly short. "Yet forty days and Nineveh shall be overthrown." Whether this is the entirety of Jonah's message or not, we do not know. What is interesting is that there is no reason given for the pronouncement of their impending doom nor is there a call to repentance. In other words, this is one of the worst sermons recorded in scripture. Regardless, the Ninevites sincerely repent.

Jonah is not pleased with the outcome. This outcome is why Jonah fled in the first place. He knew he would pronounce

---

57 Tremper Longman III and David E. Garland, *Expositor's Bible Commentary: Daniel–Malachi* Grand Rapids: Zondervan, 2008), 475.

a message of doom, they would repent, and God would relent. In chapter four he is so angry that God has relented he wants his own life to end.

I love how the book ends. God asks Jonah, "…should I not have concern for the great city of Nineveh, in which there are more than a hundred and twenty thousand people who cannot tell their right hand from their left—and also many animals?"[58] I love this verse because it reveals a God who is concerned with people's destiny. No matter who they are or how deserving they are of punishment, he desires that people experience redemption. I also find it revealing of God's heart that he mentions the animals too.

Another interesting little detail about this narrative is that Jonah's own people were living in disobedience. Israel is as deserving—if not more because she should know better—of judgment as Assyria. The justice Jonah desired to be dealt out to Nineveh is the same justice his own people deserved. However, Jonah would likely appeal to God's compassionate grace on behalf of Israel while desiring that same compassionate grace be denied his enemies.

Taking Justice Into Our Own Hands

We have an infinite capacity to embrace bias in regards to our own deservedness of judgment, and a limited capacity to see others as deserving of grace. This makes us unfit to sit in the judge's seat. So the answer to the question I posed earlier—Should we take justice in our own hands?—is not just no, but the answer is

---

[58] Jonah 4:11

that it is actually impossible for us to take justice into our own hands. As soon as we take justice into our own hands, it ceases to be truly and purely just.

Any effort to distribute justice will simply tip the scales in the other direction. Our efforts to execute justice perpetually add to the injustice in our world because we are sinful. We are broken. We are desperately selfish. Whatever it is we take in our own hands to balance the scales, we can be sure that it is not justice.

Reflection/Discussion Questions

1. Why do you think we are prone to excusing our mistakes and wrong actions while desiring the full measure of justice for the mistakes and wrong actions of others?

2. Can you think of a time when you were ungracious with someone for a mistake, wrongful action, or error that you yourself were guilty of committing?

3. Anthony suggested that our attempts to exact justice will always be biased and therefore will actually add to and perpetuate injustice. Do you agree or disagree? Why or why not?

4. Jonah was called by God to go preach to his political, national, religious, and ethnic enemies with the complete awareness that God's grace and compassion would be extended to them should they repent. Who are the "Ninevites" in your life? The people who have hurt you or are positioned as your enemy. Who are your political, religious, and ethnic "enemies"?

5. Do you believe in your heart of hearts that "they" are as deserving of God's grace and compassion as you are?

CHAPTER 7
Lots of Pages

My wife has this uncanny ability to forget things that don't really matter, which is a gift. She's not one of those women who holds onto things, remembering for years and years the offenses committed against her. So many of the stereotypes about men and women do not fit us. I am the verbal processor who wants to process my "feelings." She doesn't like to talk and talk and talk. I have a hard time not holding onto hurts. She can move on to the next thing like nothing ever happened. She is more gracious and much more forgiving than I am.

As I said in the last chapter, I want justice *and compensation*. When people hurt me, I want them to understand the gravity of what they have done. I want them to pay for it. Don't misunderstand what I mean. I don't want something terrible to happen to them. I just want them to be emotionally distraught and sorrowful for hurting me.

If you are married, you can probably imagine how problematic an expectation like this can be within the marriage. Married people have given their hearts to another imperfect person. That person has the most vulnerable access to the other's heart. Meaning, they also have the most opportunity to make a mess of things by hurting the other person. Grace and forgiveness in marriage are absolute necessities for a healthy relationship. My wife has done a much better job of modeling forgiveness towards me than I have towards her.

One example rises to the top. There have been several times in our marriage that I have done something stupid. Something for which Emily had every right to be angry with me. One particular time, after I had done something stupid and hurtful, I was sulking in my own shame. This wasn't the first time I had done the same stupid thing. I felt worthless. I felt like a failure. I felt like she should be angry with me for days—maybe even forever actually. We were driving in the car as I sat in silence and shame.

Emily looked over and asked what was wrong. I expressed how terrible I felt and how guilty I felt. She looked over and said to me, "Today is a new day. We are turning a new page."

As I said, this wasn't the first time I had done something that hurt her in this way. So, I remember saying to her, "Again, we are turning a new page *again*."

What she said after has been seared into my memory as one of the most grace-filled and powerful statements she has ever said to me. Calmly, but with authority, she declared over me, "It is ok, our book has lots of pages."

He Must Die

Over two thousand years ago one of the most corrupt and rigged executions took place in the Roman occupied territory of Palestine. There was a man, a rabbi, who had developed a significant following of people. People were heralding him as the Jewish promised Messiah. Our modern understanding of the term "Messiah" is extremely tainted with our Christian hindsight. To us today, Messiah means "Savior," but during First Century Palestine it meant "king."

By the turn of the first century, hopes in Israel for a Messiah were high. Israel had once again come under the rule of a foreign nation. The Jewish people were under the rule of the Roman Empire. Contrary to most conquered peoples, the Jewish people refused to adopt the Greco-Roman culture. Most conquered nations did not have a problem with Hellenization (imposed Greek Culture); they simply synchronized the Greek culture with their own. For the faithful Jew, synchronization was not an option.

Hellenization was a bitter reminder of a time before the Roman Empire when the Seleucid king, Antiochus IV Epiphanes, tried to force Greek culture upon the Jewish people. A couple centuries before the Roman Empire rose to power most of the known world had come under the rule of Alexander the Great. After Alexander's untimely death, his empire was up for grabs and fought over by four of his generals. Two dynasties prevailed in the aftermath: the Ptolemaic Dynasty which ruled from 305 – 30 BC and the Seleucid Dynasty which ruled from

312 – 63 BC. Antiochus IV Epiphanes was a Seleucid King who ruled over Palestine from 175 -164 BC.

In an effort to homogenize his kingdom and with absolute disdain for the Jewish culture, he outlawed circumcision, Sabbath observance, Jewish festivals, and Jewish temple rituals. The ultimate disgrace came after Antiochus invaded the Most Holy Place of the temple and sacrificed an unclean pig to the Greek god, Zeus (December 167 BC). This act pushed the Jewish people over the edge, and the Maccabean revolt ensued.

> "On the twenty-fifth of December, 164 BC, three years to the day from Antiochus's desecration of the temple, Judah Maccabee rode into Jerusalem to shouts of 'hosanna' and the waving of palm branches. He cleansed the temple, removing from it the images of Greek gods, the foreign altars, and the other despised trappings of pagan worship, and rededicated the whole of the temple to the Lord."[59]

For almost a century, the Jewish people held off the Greek armies and established their independence. During this time, the forerunners to the Pharisees focused on preserving the Law and their religious traditions.[60]

---

[59] Bartholomew and Goheen, *The Drama of Scripture: Finding our Place in the Biblical Story*, 127.

[60] Bartholomew and Goheen, *The Drama of Scripture: Finding our Place in the Biblical Story*, 127-129.

In 63 BC, Pompey the Great expanded the Roman Empire to Palestine. Now, under the Roman Empire, the Jewish people were ruled by client kings and governors who were ultimately subject to Rome. Against Rome's desired outcome, the Jewish people were allowed to practice their religion, but they were under strict watch. There was peace in Palestine, but it was a very fragile peace. Any sign of an uprising could result in the invasion of Roman Legions and the sure massacre of those intending to rebel. By New Testament times, racial hatred and Messianic anticipation was high.

There were a number of individuals who claimed Messiahship, but all of them were silenced by Rome. There was even a group of guerrilla terrorists known as Zealots. They were political activists who favored armed revolt against Rome. Some extreme groups of Zealots participated in political acts of terrorism against Rome. They were called "Zealots" because they believed they were "zealous" for God's Law and for social justice and national liberation.

As I said, there was "peace" in the Palestinian province, but it was very fragile. The Jewish leaders were well aware of the fragility of their freedoms. While these Zealots and "Messiah" figures thought they were helping usher in God's promised liberation, they were actually just a headache to Rome. Like an annoying fly that if it persists will simply need to be squashed.

So, when a Galilean rabbi came into Jerusalem for Passover to shouts of "Hosanna" and "Blessed is the coming Kingdom," the Pharisees, Sanhedrin leaders, and the High Priest were quite alarmed. This rabbi was stirring up a mob of frustrated nationalists who sincerely believed he was the "Messiah." The Pharisees, Scribes, and teachers of the Law wanted him silenced because he posed a threat to the freedoms they were permitted. If the Roman officials stationed in Jerusalem at the time viewed this rabbi as a threat to the Empire, the whole nation could suffer. Additionally, the Jewish leaders benefited from their cooperation with Rome. This rabbi was a threat to their freedoms and the little power they did hold.

He also was clearly not the "Messiah" because he associated with the unclean and the distasteful. The people heralded him as a great teacher and a powerful man of God, but no man of God would eat and associate with the kinds of people this man associated with. He was misleading the people, degrading their traditions, and robbing them of their influence. He had to be silenced. He had to be killed.

They couldn't execute him in their own power—they had to go to the Roman authorities to carry out such a punishment. So, they paid one of his followers to betray him, set up a mock trial, and leveraged the chaos of a mob to get their way. This rabbi was sentenced to be crucified.

He was mocked, beaten, and flogged. A Roman flogging is no light matter. His body was lacerated by the Roman whip until it was hardly recognizable as human. Then he was crucified. Crucifixion stands in history as an example of humanity's horrifying capacity to think up brutal ways to kill one another.

Victims of crucifixion were stripped naked and nailed or tied by their hands and feet to a wooden cross. If nailed, the 7-inch spike would cause severe nerve damage in both the hands and feet. Their outstretched arms sustained the weight of their hanging bodies and their bodyweight would suspend their diaphragm in a perpetual state of inhalation. In order to exhale, the victim would have to pull themselves up using the very arms that had been impaled. Usually, victims of crucifixion would die from a asphyxiation.

One Roman Senator and lawyer once stated, "The very word 'cross' should be far removed not only from the person of a Roman citizen, but from his thoughts, his eyes and his ears. For it is not merely the actual occurrence of these things but the very mention of them that is unworthy of a Roman citizen or a free man."[61] Crucifixion was reserved for slaves and the worst of criminals. It was a shameful and dishonorable way to die.

This man, the one who had made the lame walk and the blind see, the one who had raised the dead and exercised authority over demons, in the midst of this great injustice, this horrific agony, and utter humiliation uttered these words:

> "Father, forgive them, for they do not know what they are doing."[62]

---

[61] Campbell, N. (2013). Cicero (and Paul) on the cross. Retrieved August 08, 2020, from https://st-eutychus.com/2013/cicero-and-paul-on-the-cross/

[62] Luke 23:34

The Way of the Cross

This man was, of course, our Lord and Savior Jesus Christ. The one we proclaim to worship and the one whose life and teachings we claim to follow. The one who called us to love our enemies, do good to those who hurt us, and to pray for those who would persecute us. He was betrayed by a close friend, falsely accused, horrifically beaten, publicly humiliated, and brutally executed. Yet, in the face of all this, he had the audacity to declare, "Father, forgive…" Who? The very people who were just driving the nails into his hands.

I don't know about you, but this is just crazy. When you stop and think about the gravity of what is happening in that little snippet of Scripture, it is quite overwhelming. Jesus is God. Jesus is the exact representation of God.[63] When God is being killed, he utters with his dying breath… a declaration of forgiveness. A declaration that has the extraordinary authority, weight, and power of the voice that spoke the universe into existence.

For a minute, I want you to try to lay aside your Christian systematic theologies and Sunday School answers and recognize the irony of what is taking place on the cross. So often we only see the cross through the lens of sacrifice and substitution. There is more going on here. While the human narrative of securing power is attempting to make an example out of this Jewish rabbi, the God of the universe is showing us the only way to disarm corrupt power and systemic evil.

---

[63] Hebrews 1:3

The cross was a warning. People were crucified in public just outside the city so that people who entered or left the city would be reminded of who was in control. It wasn't about justice. It was about power and domination. Rome is an archetypical example of the human narrative of power. Rome typifies how we believe victory is secured: the worldly, human way of winning is through the exertion of superior force by means of violence if necessary.

Whether it is nations fighting against one another in an attempt to secure international superiority or coworkers violently attacking one another's reputations, the way we "win" in this life is through the exertion of our power over another. This, of course, is not the way of the cross. Paul writes, "He forgave us all our sins, having canceled the charge of our legal indebtedness, which stood against us and condemned us; he has taken it away, nailing it to the cross. And having disarmed the *powers* and *authorities*, he made a public spectacle of *them*, triumphing over them by the cross."[64]

As we discovered in the last chapter, our attempts to rectify the wrongs done against us through revenge will never truly balance the scales. We cannot distribute justice and it remain justice. Similarly, we cannot right the wrongs in the world by waging war as the world does. The correction and making right of the evil in our world will never come through Christians securing influence in the political arena. It will never come through military conquest of communist dictatorships. It will never come by winning arguments and debates with atheists.

[64] Colossians 2:13-15

It will never come through social media rants and witty but rude memes. It will never come through isolationism—as if God's greatest desire for us is to await our evacuation in our "holy huddles."

I was never good at science, but I remember there being this law that goes like this "for every action there is an equal and opposite reaction." So many of our efforts to usher in God's Kingdom simply create and contribute to the reactions that perpetuate evil. *Evil is triumphed when it is absorbed by love and transformed through resurrection.* The way we absorb evil and transform it is through forgiveness. Forgiveness is the way of the cross, and therefore the way of the Christ-follower.

The Unreasonableness of Forgiveness

Unforgiveness is just, fair, and rational in most situations. The genocidal dictator doesn't *deserve* forgiveness. The unfaithful spouse doesn't *deserve* forgiveness. The rapist, thief, and murderer don't *deserve* forgiveness. Forgiveness is counterintuitive. Forgiveness even feels wrong at times. Yet, if we claim to follow Christ, forgiveness is non-negotiable.

Philip Yancey wrote, "The gospel of grace begins and ends with forgiveness."[65] Forgiveness is the only remedy for the cancerous root of ungracious bitterness. Forgiveness is unnatural—everything in us wants revenge, vindication, and retribution. We want justice our way and often through our means. So, we manipulate, scheme, avoid, gossip, retaliate, sabotage, and

---

[65] Philip Yancey, *What's So Amazing about Grace* (Grand Rapids: Zondervan , 1997), 96.

execute our own forms of justice and revenge. The problem with this is that it stands in direct opposition to the gospel.[66]

You have not truly embraced the grace of God's forgiveness if you harbor the capacity to withhold it from someone else. Actually, you cannot receive the grace of God's forgiveness if you withhold grace and forgiveness from others.[67] I heard a preacher once say that "We are never more like God than when we forgive." I think this is true. I think it means we are also never more unlike God than when we don't forgive.

Knowing that through forgiveness I reflect God doesn't make it any easier. I love what Henri Nouwen wrote about this topic of forgiveness:

> I have often said, 'I forgive you,' but even as I said these words my heart remained angry or resentful. I still wanted to hear the story that tells me that I was right after all; I still wanted to hear apologies and excuses; I still wanted the satisfaction of receiving some praise in return—if only the praise for being so forgiving!

> But God's forgiveness is unconditional; it comes from a heart that does not demand anything for itself, a heart that is completely empty of self-seeking. It is this divine forgiveness that I have to practice in my daily life. It calls me to keep

---

[66] Matt. 6:14, Col. 3:13, Eph. 4:32

[67] Heb. 12:15, Matt. 6:9-14

stepping over all my arguments that say forgiveness is unwise, unhealthy and impractical. It challenges me to step over all my needs for gratitude and compliments. Finally, it demands of me that I step over that wounded part of my heart that feels hurt and wronged and that wants to stay in control and put a few conditions between me and the one whom I am asked to forgive.[68]

Maybe this is what Jesus meant when he said we have to pick up our cross. Forgiveness requires the crucifixion of our very selves. It means relinquishing the desire to control what happens to the other person.

Transforming Power of Forgiveness

How can we though? How can we just let people off the hook who don't deserve it? How can we forgive?

One word—transformation. This is the gospel, this is the good news—that transformation, that resurrection is possible. That in Christ, your heart can be so radically changed that you can have a new capacity to love, to serve, to forgive, to give, to sacrifice. I am, in the face of a world torn by violence, hate, and chaos, bold enough to believe that the gospel can change a human heart. That through Christ we are new creations with a new capacity to fully love God and others.

---

[68] Henri J. M. Nouwen, *The Return of the Prodigal Son: A Story of Homecoming* (New York: Doubleday, 1992), 129-130.

How can we experience this transformation? God is the one who works in us. His Spirit alive in us is the only hope we have for real, genuine change. We cannot try hard enough, do good enough, or perform holy enough to make this happen. We cannot manufacture transformation, but we can allow the opportunity for God to work. What is more, we can actually invite him to move and work in our lives. There is an element of Divine/Human cooperation to this transformative work.

We can't make transformation happen in our own power, but, we can hinder God's part by holding on to bitterness. Unforgiveness fundamentally blocks transformation. Unforgiveness harbors resentment, which by definition requires that you re-live and re-feel the past. Transformation is by nature a change. Re-living the past hinders change and therefore prevents transformation. Not only that, resentment and bitterness and unforgiveness create a toxic environment in the soul of a person that is conducive to all sorts of enslaving thought patterns.

Withholding forgiveness actually enslaves our souls. It's like there is a spiritual law of redemption in which our own freedom and healing are intrinsically connected to our releasing other people.

We have to release our pride, our right to be right, and our need to execute justice. The remedy is almost underwhelming because it sounds so simple, but the execution is anything but simple. We have to release, surrender, let go. For me, this has looked like a process of asking God to help me heal from a hurt or wound while declaring, "I forgive them."

The process of forgiveness has looked like surrendering the thoughts of vengeance or retribution that fire across my synapses. You know the ones? Those thoughts where you fantasize about someone hurting them the way they hurt you. Or, thoughts of them having a very public and epic failure. Or, those times you almost rejoice when trials assail their life. When those thoughts start to come, I try to shut them down rather than entertain them. The process of forgiveness and the transformation that God does happens in our interior lives.

The hardest part about letting go and forgiving is that we feel justice will go unmet. We often feel like forgiveness condones the other person's actions. I think for most of us the most difficult thing to get over is the feeling that we are "letting them off the hook." The opposite is actually true. Forgiveness by nature means that what the person did was *wrong* or else forgiveness would not be necessary. Forgiveness doesn't condone the wrong actions of others. It actually requires that we call it like it is—what the other person did was wrong.

Forgiveness is an act of letting go so that we can receive. So long as we are holding onto the noose of another person we cannot receive the lifeline God offers to us. Forgiveness also refuses to allow the hurt in our souls to spoil and turn toxic. Forgiveness forces us to address the hurt with authenticity rather than conceal our wound until it is so infected it needs to be amputated. When we harbor our wounds and refuse to allow Christ to heal them, our sinful propensities take over infecting the wound and ultimately killing something vital in our souls.

The other hurdle many of us have to get over is the issue of reconciliation. Forgiveness is not reconciliation, nor does it require it. Sometimes reconciliation would be dangerous. Some victims should never face their assailants on this side of heaven.

There are also times when forgiveness is offered but not received. We can't force others to be reconciled to us. Forgiveness is a divine transaction in which we turn over the person's debt against us to God. When we do this, a miracle happens. We are free to love as God loves.

While reconciliation is not the same as forgiveness and while it is not always possible, reconciliation in many cases should be pursued. My undergraduate theology professor, Dr. Chris Bounds, describes love as "the desire for union—oneness and fellowship, *and* it is the choices we make to bring that about. It is the working of the desire and the will together to experience oneness." In other words, loving our enemies is not just some sort of idealistic philosophy that we simply affirm in our Sunday School classrooms. Loving our enemies, as Christ calls us to, should actually affect our desires and our will to act.

This kind of love, this radical act of forgiveness, is a miracle. Forgiving others their wrongs against us requires resurrection level transformation. But, Paul wrote in his letter to the Romans that "The Spirit of God, *who raised Jesus from the dead, lives in you....*"[69] The Good News is about more than your one-way ticket to the good place. The Good News is that, through the power of the Holy Spirit, there is resurrection

---

[69] Romans 8:11

happening in your soul every day. Every day you die to your sinful self a resurrection happens. Remember, resurrection can only happen if something has died. If you want to deal a death blow to sin and darkness and evil in the world around you, then start asking the Holy Spirit to help you forgive everyone always.

Forgiving everyone always includes yourself. So many people I have encountered in ministry haven't forgiven themselves for their past sins. I have ministered to parent's who blamed themselves for trauma their children experienced by another family member. They feel like they should have known or done something. I've seen divorcees, moms who have had abortions, and individuals who struggled with addiction struggle to actually forgive themselves.

Their unforgiveness of themselves obstructs the free flow of God's transforming forgiveness in their lives. This happens because we are presuming to stand in God's place as judge. We presume to have a better sense of justice than God when we hold sins against ourselves that God has already forgiven. Receiving and believing in his justification means believing his redefinition of your identity as "not guilty" is true.

Forgive everyone always. When we participate in acts of gracious forgiveness, we defy and suffocate the powers of resentment and bitterness that threaten to poison our souls. God has a book with lots of pages, perhaps we need to start writing a book with the people around us that has lots of pages.

Reflection/Discussion Questions

1. Have you ever been graciously forgiven by someone (other than God)? How did their forgiveness impact you?

2. Why is the forgiveness that Jesus taught and modeled such a radical idea?

3. If we think of forgiveness as a process of letting go and surrendering, what are the things we have to let go of? Our pride? Our hurt? The other person? Make as comprehensive of a list as you can.

4. How do you know when you have forgiven someone? What sort of evidence or fruit is produced in your heart and soul?

5. When and how should we pursue reconciliation? When is reconciliation not possible?

6. Anthony suggested that part of forgiveness involves us forgiving ourselves. Are there areas of your life where you might be refusing to receive grace from God because you are refusing to forgive yourself? What would it look like for you to forgive yourself?

CHAPTER 8
Planks and Specks

Have you ever seen the *Princess Bride?* If you haven't, you should stop what you are doing right now and watch it. It is a classic romantic comedy and one of the best of all time in my humble opinion. My humble opinion is right though and validated by Rotten Tomatoes which gives the movie a 97%. Anyhow, there's a popular meme that has circulated around the internet based on a quote from one of the characters.

One of the "bad guys" in the story believes himself to be a genius. Yet, with all his intelligence, his plans keep getting foiled. To which he responds by saying, "Inconceivable!" My favorite character, Inigo Montoya, is not really a good guy or bad guy but a guy on a personal mission to avenge his father's death. In one scene, after the super genius has again repeated his refrain "Inconceivable," Inigo Montoya looks at him and says, "You keep using that word. I do not think it means what you think it means."

The meme on the internet has a picture of Inigo Montoya with that phrase or some version of it. A popular "Christian" meme (whatever that is) changes the wording a little bit. The

Christian version goes like this, "You keep using that Bible verse. I do not think it means what you think it means." The meme is a passive-aggressive way to call out the Biblical error of others.

On Facebook, I recently saw this meme used regarding the verse about judging others. You can find it in Matthew 7. Jesus tells his listeners to not judge others for they will be judged according to the standard by which they judge. The meme was intending to call out the tendency of people to use this verse out of context as a force field shielding them from any accountability. Some people appeal to this verse—"You can't judge me"—to justify their sinful behaviors. However, the meme was off-putting to me because it represents the other extreme. Some Christians appeal to Scriptures about "knowing their fruit" or "using discernment" to justify all sorts of judgmental opinions about others.

Categories and Golden Retrievers

Why is it so easy to judge other people? I can hardly go to the mall without finding myself "people watching." Some of the time my observations are innocent, but other times I find myself making judgments about people I don't even know. The worst is when I observe something that I disapprove of and my facial expression gives it away. My wife says that I can't hide what I'm thinking.

All of us make sense of the world by interpreting our experiences and interactions. Our brains are hardwired to categorize everything from inanimate objects to the motives behind people's actions. All the information we audibly, visually, and physically interact with is translated by this process of categorization, and many times the process happens automatically without much thought or reflection.

My wife loves dogs. As a kid, she would study dog books—books that had pictures and details about a variety of dog species. She memorized quite a bit of information about all sorts of things concerning dogs. For some species, she knows what kind of temperament they have, what their average life span is, and whether or not that species is characterized by any specific health concerns. She's like a walking dog encyclopedia. So, it is rare that we see a dog in the park that she doesn't recognize, but it happens. When it happens, she usually asks the owner, "What kind of dog is this?"

What is happening there on a cognitive level is that she is visually seeing a characteristic that doesn't fit into one of her categories. Her brain quickly and effortlessly went through this process: "you are seeing an animal and it is a dog." Normally her brain can quickly determine what kind of dog. "You are seeing a Golden Retriever." When she sees something about the build or the coat that doesn't have a category, her brain can't file it appropriately and it raises the question: What kind of dog is this? Usually, the dog is some sort of mixed breed.

Our brains do this with objects, animals, people, and even intentions. Our brains observe people's actions and then make assumptions about the person's intent. Our assumptions about their intent usually lead to judgments about their character. Again, we do so much of this effortlessly and without thoughtful reflection.

For example, let's say your spouse leaves their dishes in the sink. You've told them that this frustrates you and even adds to your stress levels. They know you feel more at peace when things are clean and tidy. Rather than giving them the benefit of the doubt, you will most likely assume that they deliberately left the dishes in the sink to tick you off. What you will probably not do is reflect on the reason they may have left them in the sink. Maybe they were running late. Maybe they just forgot and slipped into an old habit. Instead of leaving room for the possibility of human error, you will jump to the conclusion that they don't respect you or your preferences.

We make value judgments about people's motives based on what we infer from their observed actions all the time. When our assumptions about people create a misunderstanding, conflict often results. While it is natural and even helpful that our brains can process information so automatically, it can become problematic when we have narrow categories. When we don't know the whole story, our assumptions will likely leave something out. We will likely make judgments about people that are based on inadequate information.

So, since I am not a neuroscientist or a psychologist, I cannot explain all the intricacies of how the brain categorizes life and which parts of the brain actually light up on a functional Magnetic Resonance Imaging (fMRI) when processing this information. My point is simply that we judge people because that's how our brains interact with the world. The problem is not our brain's process. The problem is our tendency to turn these stereotypical categories into transcendent truths about other people's value. This problem is further complicated by our lack of exposure to things that challenge our categories.

Cultural Awareness & A Single Story

The lens through which we see the world is greatly shaped by our cultural upbringing. "We're socialized into our respective cultures first and foremost through the family setting. This socialization is further reinforced through school, the media, church, and eventually through our professional networks and environments."[70] Our cultural perspectives influence everything from dialect to brand preferences. It is amazing how opinionated people can be about Ford versus Chevy.

People's views on many things are not really based on concrete, factual evidence. I think Wendy's is better than McDonald's. Someone else may think McDonald's is better than Wendy's. Is this right, wrong, or just different? Yet, we can get extremely passionate about brands, sports teams, and political views. Some of the things we are passionate about are really not right or wrong issues. Yet we fight as if they are life and death issues.

I remember playing sports in high school. Grown adults would scream and yell at other adolescent teens on the other team emphatically declaring their inferiority. Why? Was it

---

[70] David Livermore, *Cultural Intelligence* (Grand Rapids: Baker Academic, 2009), 87.

because they actually knew the character of the other kid? No. It was simply because they were from the rival school. We have a tendency to believe *our way* of seeing things is *the way*, and we use all sorts of combative tactics to express the superiority of our view.

David Livermore explains in his book *Cultural Intelligence* how our tendency to see things a certain way fails to take into account the possibility that the way other people do things could just be different. He talks about how we tend to categorize life according to narrow or wide categories:

> "Narrow categorizers focus on differences... Narrow categorizers watch the behavior of people from different cultures and categorize them based on what those actions would mean in one's own cultural context. A narrow categorizer has sub-conscious lists that include words that should be used by educated people, clothes that shouldn't appear on Christians, and norms for how married couples should relate...Those with narrow category width are much quicker to characterize things as right versus wrong."[71]

In other words, narrow categorizers have a tendency to view things that are different as if they are wrong.

This is problematic considering the diversity of cultures present in our world. If we are not careful, we can make the

---

[71] Livermore, *Cultural Intelligence*, 179.

mistake of categorizing the way other cultures do things as being wrong. When, as Christians, we interpret "wrong" as also sinful we can find ourselves condemning entire groups of people for things God hasn't condemned. This happened when Western missionaries evangelized the Native Americans. Christianizing the Natives was viewed as synonymous with Westernizing and civilizing them. Elements of their cultural identity were condemned that could have been redeemed.

Our narrow categories can cause us to judge people based on a "single story." For one of my seminary courses, I had to watch several TED talks. If you haven't watched any TED talks, I highly recommend that you do. One of the most impactful TED talks I had to view was by Nigerian novelist, Chimamanda Ngozi Adichie, on "The danger of a single story." The premise is that we often reduce people to the limited details we know about their story. We paint them with a single story.

Here is an excerpt from the video transcript:

> "I come from a conventional, middle-class Nigerian family. My father was a professor. My mother was an administrator. And so we had, as was the norm, live-in domestic help, who would often come from nearby rural villages. So, the year I turned eight, we got a new house boy. His name was Fide. The only thing my mother told us about him was that his family was very poor....

Then one Saturday, we went to his village to visit, and his mother showed us a beautifully patterned basket made of dyed raffia that his brother had made. I was startled. It had not occurred to me that anybody in his family could actually make something. All I had heard about them was how poor they were, so that it had become impossible for me to see them as anything else but poor. Their poverty was my single story of them.

Years later, I thought about this when I left Nigeria to go to university in the United States. I was 19. My American roommate was shocked by me. She asked where I had learned to speak English so well, and was confused when I said that Nigeria happened to have English as its official language. She asked if she could listen to what she called my "tribal music," and was consequently very disappointed when I produced my tape of Mariah Carey.

...What struck me was this: She had felt sorry for me even before she saw me. Her default position toward me, as an African, was a kind of patronizing, well-meaning pity. My roommate had a single story of Africa: a single story of catastrophe. In this single story, there was no possibility of Africans being similar to her in any way, no possibility of feelings more complex than pity, no possibility of a connection as human equals."[72]

Have you ever painted someone with a single story? Have you ever allowed your narrow categorization and your single story narrative to actually determine the value of another person?

When I was a kid I somehow came to believe that smoking tobacco was bad and not something "good" Christians should do. I still think smoking is not ideal, wise, or healthy. However, I had a tendency of assuming people who smoked not only were not Christians but *could not be* Christians. I had a single story for smokers and I was a narrow categorizer. Sometimes how we paint people of a different race, religion, or political view reduces them to a single story.

I have the belief that this is something we are prone to do. We see the addict only through the lens of their addiction, we see the pregnant teen only through the lens of her naïve mistake, we see the illegal immigrant only through the lens of our narrative we have constructed about immigrants—single stories.

One of the things that breaks the boundaries of our single stories is relationship. I used to have all sorts of negative assumptions about homeless people until I actually talked with someone at a homeless shelter. *Face to face interaction with*

---

[72] Chimamanda Ngozi Adichie. 2009. "The Danger of a Single Story." Ted.com. TED Talks. 2009. https://www.ted.com/talks/chimamanda_adichie_the_danger_of_a_single_story.

people who are created in the image of God has a way of changing our hearts. It also has a way of adding dimension to our single stories and broadening our narrow categorization.

Like A Child

Several years ago I connected with our local homeless shelter to be a "discipler" in their self-sufficiency program. The homeless shelter is an unashamedly Christian organization. Part of their program involves residents being paired one on one with a "discipler" and going through a three-year process and several different bible studies. A lot never make it through the whole three-year process. Residents move out, get kicked out, or leave for several reasons.

For almost a year I was paired up with a guy we will call Rick. Rick was a recovering drug addict, but he was a believer. He was from Utah and grew up in the Mormon faith. Much of his experience in the Mormon faith was tainted by legalism. So, when he encountered the Good News of salvation by grace through faith, he "converted" to the Protestant faith.

Early in his life, Rick found himself caught up in the wrong crowd and pursuing the wrong things. Rick is now in his early fifties and living in a transitional living facility. Rick and I spent a lot of time together one on one. I came to realize that Rick battled with a lot of shame. Even though he didn't believe God was legalistic and impossible to please, he struggled with his own vices. Fear and shame were weapons the enemy would often use against Rick.

Rick loves Jesus though. I have no doubt about it. Rick also has a compassion for people that rivals that of a lot of more "holy" Christians I have met. Rick was always helping people. While he was at the shelter, he was one of the few who had a vehicle. So he was always giving people rides to help them out.

After Rick and I had spent months meeting together, I invited him over to our home for dinner. Our son was almost two at the time. I remember Rick sitting at our kitchen table making small talk with me and my wife when our son walked up to him and climbed in his lap. This was the first time my son had ever met Rick. I was overwhelmed with the reality that our toddler treated Rick like any other person in his life. He made absolutely no value judgments about Rick. He didn't care that Rick struggled with addiction. He didn't care that Rick was homeless.

Rick was a bit surprised too. The smile on Rick's face was priceless. In that moment, I couldn't help but feel like my son embodied the childlike faith necessary for the Kingdom of God that Jesus talked about (Matt. 18:3). My son acknowledged the basic human dignity of a person that many people might judge as being someone to avoid.

Planks and Specks

Jesus teaches us not to judge our fellow man or else we too will be judged according to the standard by which we judged others. Some people appeal to this Scripture to justify living without any moral restraint. The heart of these people is oftentimes as abrasive as those who would judge them. The sentiment behind "God is my judge" often comes across like this: "Back the (cuss word) off! You have no right to hold me accountable!" I don't think this is what Jesus had in mind when he spoke this teaching to his listeners.

However, many people seem to get really hung up on defending the truth and holding other people accountable. First of all, truth, if it is true, doesn't need our defense. Secondly, people who are overly obsessed with correcting others miss the heart of this passage too.

I think Jesus is saying that if we judge other people without having a heart full of grace, compassion, and love, then we better watch out because God will judge us according to that standard instead of according to the standard of the cross. Paul wrote to the believers at Ephesus to "speak the truth in love."[73] So often, I think people get hung up on just speaking the truth. You can't speak the truth in love to someone whose story you don't know. You can't speak the truth in love by lambasting people on Twitter, Facebook, or a blog page. You can't speak the truth in love through a meme that makes fun of atheists, people who identify as LGBTQ, or Muslims.

Jesus goes on to say that we need to first remove the plank from our own eyes before we attempt to remove the speck in someone else's eyes. I used to believe the analogy of plank and speck had to do with the size of the sin. Some sins are "specks" and other sins are "planks." I have found that in the church we sometimes have a list of sins on the "plank list." I have also found that we tend to feel quite comfortable harboring condemning and judgmental attitudes towards those "plank" sins.

---

[73] Ephesians 4:15

Which is ironic because I have also heard that sin is sin in God's eyes.

I don't think Jesus was talking about the size of the sin. If you have a plank in your eye then it obscures your ability to see anything clearly, let alone your neighbor's sin. I think Jesus was warning us to self-reflect and make sure we have clarity. Both on our own motives and the sin of the other person. If you don't have clarity on your own sin and your own motives then you have no business presuming to have the clarity to fix the speck in your neighbor's eye.

When it comes to judging people, I think a distinction needs to be made between judgment that results in wise discernment versus judgment that presumes to hold the gavel. Only God holds the gavel. I also think there is a difference between judging people to assess their level of "spiritual-ness" and exercising the sort of intuition that knows a friend needs accountability.

My best friend in high school had a season of life when he wasn't making the best decisions. I had the discernment and good judgment to know that some of his choices weren't life-giving in the long run. However, I was never judgmental towards him. I spoke truth to him when he opened up and shared things with me. I think part of the reason we are still best friends today is that he knew I loved him and wanted God's best for him.

I think there are two things we should keep in mind when it comes to exercising our judgment with other people. First, we need to thoughtfully and prayerfully reflect on our own hearts. This isn't just about reflecting on whether we have some obvious, un-repented sin in our lives. This is about reflecting on our motives for even wanting to address the issues of other people. If there is even an ounce of self-righteous pride or personal satisfaction in pointing out the error in someone else then we've missed Jesus' point. We can be sure we have plank-itis in our eye. Keep in mind also that "plankitis" is contagious. Usually transferred via gossip mouth.

Secondly, removing something from someone's eye assumes close proximity. We cannot remove a speck from our neighbor's eye from a distance. Likewise, speaking the truth in love assumes relationship. I find it a good rule of thumb to allow my relationship with people to determine the level of accountability I exercise with them. If our desire truly is to correct people for fear that their choices are destructive, then our desire would also be to truly walk with them in *relationship*.

Lastly, I think it is worth mentioning that I believe we have no business judging the world by the standard of the gospel. Someone who doesn't follow Christ has not committed to the standards of following Christ. It's like holding someone who doesn't work for "XYZ Inc." accountable to the company's dress code policy. They don't work for the company, therefore they can't be held accountable to the company's policy.

Christians get really hung up on calling out the sinfulness of the world. Those homosexuals, Muslims, and liberals are sinners! And, we often feel obliged to make that abundantly clear to them. This is often fruitless and only comes across as hateful and judgmental. Here's the thing, Paul wrote to the church at

Corinth that the person without the Holy Spirit does not understand the spiritual truth the Spirit reveals. In fact, Paul says *"he cannot understand"* because the Spirit is the one who reveals it.[74]

Think about that. You can preach and admonish the secular world until you are blue in the face. Unless the Holy Spirit convicts and convinces it will be to no avail. I believe preaching about sin is necessary. But, I preach about it as if we are all on equal playing ground. I don't get on a soapbox condemning the world to hell. I try to be consistent with my preaching on sin. I believe stepping on toes is an equal opportunity. I try to step on the believer's toes just as much as I do an unbeliever's.

Consistently preaching about sin is important, but harping on the liberal sins of the secularist in a judgmental way is usually counterproductive to the gospel of grace. Again, I appeal to Paul so that you may know I am not just sharing my own opinions. He writes to the church at Corinth again saying, "What business is it of mine to judge those outside the church? Are you not to judge those inside?"[75]

So, when our thoughts are consumed by value judgments and moral assessments about other people, we need to look in the mirror and make sure our eyes are clear. We need to consider where all those judgments are coming from. Are they coming from a heart filled with love and grace? Or, are they coming from a place of self-righteous pride? Are we genuinely concerned for the wholeness of the other person, or are we simply comparing ourselves so that we feel vindicated?

---

[74] 1 Corinthians 2:14

[75] 1 Corinthians 5:12

Reflection/Discussion Questions

1. Can you think of some examples of how we tend to attach value to a category? (For example, if cars are a category, what factors determine the value of the car?)

2. Have you ever held an assumption or perspective about someone or a group of people that after meeting them was proven wrong? Describe what that was like.

3. How can we resist and counteract the tendency to reduce people to a single story?

4. Can you describe the difference between judging someone to assess value or to condemn versus judging someone to use discernment and wisdom?

5. How do you understand Jesus's words: "Do not judge, or you too will be judged. For in the same way you judge others, you will be judged, and with the measure you use, it will be measured to you. Why do you look at the speck of sawdust in your brother's eye and pay no attention to the plank in your own eye" (Matthew 7:1-3, NIV)?

6. How should we go about confronting sin in other people? Should we just not confront others? Is there a way to confront others with God-honoring motives? Explain.

CHAPTER 9
That Gut Feeling

A couple years ago I was leaving our driveway on my way to an important ministry appointment. As I pulled out of our driveway I saw a kitten on the road. I have a soft spot for cats. I know it is a popular thing to be a "dog person," but I grew up always having pet cats. Plus, for argument's sake, cats are easier. Cats deposit their excrement in a designated location while dogs will poop all over your yard. Cats can be left for several days with food and water while dogs can hardly be left for more than 8 hours. And, our dog has been sprayed two years in a row by a skunk because he was too dumb not to chase it. I have never owned a cat that got sprayed by a skunk. Just saying.

Anyways, back to the story. I saw a kitten on the road that looked as if it had been hit by a car. As I was thinking in my mind, "Oh, that's sad," it lifted its head up. I was shocked because I thought for sure that it was roadkill. I went from "Oh, that's sad" to "Oh! It's alive!" I parked my car back in our driveway because I hated the idea of leaving this half-dead kitten in the middle of the road to become a fleshy pancake.

As I approached this kitten it used its front legs and what mobility it had in its hind legs to scoot itself off the road into our neighbor's yard. Now, I had to go to an important ministry thing and really didn't have time to deal with this animal. So, I dumped the pathetic thing on my wife. I ran back into our house and told my wife about this cat that got hit. I figured it was going to die, but I just thought it should be put out of its misery more humanely.

My poor wife cried all the way to the vet as the pathetic thing meowed and groaned in pain all the way there. As I said, I fully expected that the thing would simply be put down humanely. So you can imagine my surprise when my wife called me and said, "The vet said he just has a broken pelvis and will live. So we're keeping him and his name is Oscar." End of discussion. Which, was also surprising because my wife is the "dog person" in the family.

I remember that evening we were looking at Oscar, and said to each other, "He's kinda cute… in an ugly sort of way." He looked like a furry version of E.T. A couple of days later he looked a little cuter and we realized his face looked so weird that first night because his head was swollen from the trauma. A broken pelvis just needs to heal on its own while you remain on bed rest. That is if you're a human. Try keeping a kitten on bed rest. We nursed Oscar back to health while he lived in our bathtub for a couple of weeks. Eventually, he started standing and taking steps.

He gradually started walking and running. But, he looked… wonky while doing it. His tail looked like it got in a fight with a mousetrap. His gate was… crooked. When he ran it looked like the earth's gravitational pull was pulling him diagonally as he ran sideways. Oscar's mostly normal, although we wonder sometimes if there was brain damage from the accident too.

What started out as a moderate feeling of compassion turned into a pet adoption. Now Oscar is part of the family. That's the thing though. Compassion often compels us to act. Even if it is just compassion for an animal. Compassion and love go hand in hand. We only have compassion when there's some sort of basic foundation of love already laid. I have a love or fondness of cats, so an injured kitten hit my soft spot.

What hits your soft spot? What compels you to act? Things that arouse our compassion say something about the things we love.

Weightier Matters

Matthew records in his gospel an encounter between Jesus and an expert in the Law.[76] The expert of the Law approaches Jesus to ask him about the greatest commandment—about which commandment has the highest priority. You have to understand that the Pharisees had taken the Mosaic Law and codified it into 613 specific commands or rules. The law was categorized according to moral laws and ceremonial laws. There were 248 positive commands (do this or do that) and 365 negative commands (do not do this or that).

These commands were also categorized according to heavier or weightier commands and lighter commands. You

---

[76] Matthew 22:35-40

see, even the Pharisees knew that no human could keep all 613 commands so they often debated about which commands were greater or heavier and thus should be more closely adhered to. God would approve of their observing the more serious commands over the less significant commands. At least, that is how they looked at it.

The expert in the Law asked Jesus which command is the most important in the Law of Moses. The Pharisees believed Jesus contradicted and even taught things beyond the Law of Moses. They likely hoped that Jesus would insert his own command as the most important. If he were to do this, he would supersede Moses and set himself up as greater than Moses. You and I have hindsight and we know that Jesus actually does have the authority to do that, but for them, this would have been an extremely blasphemous thing to do.

Jesus actually does just the opposite. He quotes Moses by quoting Deuteronomy 6:5 and Leviticus 19:18. Jesus says that the first and greatest command is "to love the Lord your God with all of your heart, with all of your soul, and with all of your mind." The word "first" here literally means "first in place or time in any succession of things."[77] Meaning there is no circumstantial situation that moves it out of first place. Jesus also describes it is the "greatest"—meaning the weightiest commandment.

---

[77] "Matthew 22 (KJV)–And Jesus answered and spake." Blue Letter Bible. Accessed 9 Sep, 2022. https://www.blueletterbible.org/kjv/mat/22/1/t_conc_951038.

He does not lump the three together by simply saying, "Love the Lord your God with all of your heart, soul, and mind." The word "all" is emphasized as it is repeated all three times. Love the Lord your God with *all* of your heart. This means all of your affections, your will, and your desire. Love the Lord with *all* of your soul. This carries the idea of loving God with all of the vitality and life and breath of your being. Love the Lord with *all* of your mind. Your intellect, your viewpoints and ways of thinking, your thoughts—love God with all of that. Love God with *all* of your all.

Jesus goes on to say that the second is equally important, or the second resembles it, reflects it, is like it. Don't miss the significance of what Jesus is saying here. *The second command is like it in weightiness.* The second command is to love your neighbor as yourself. The word "love" here is active and carries the idea of hospitality. It means to "welcome, to entertain, to be fond of, or to love dearly."[78] This really challenges the conventional idea I have heard passed around that loving people means simply not hating them.

If not hating another human being is the minimal requirement of what it means to love, then we've missed something. The love Jesus calls us to involves action that is compelled by compassion. Our love for other people is as weighty and as important as our love for God.

Love God. Love People.

---

[78] "G25–agapaō–Strong's Greek Lexicon (kjv)." Blue Letter Bible. Accessed 9 Sep, 2022. https://www.blueletterbible.org/lexicon/g25/kjv/tr/0-1/

Won't You Be My Neighbor?

Luke records a similar interaction in his gospel between Jesus and an expert in the Law.[79] The expert in the Law came to Jesus and asked him about how to inherit eternal life. Jesus knows the man is well versed in the Mosaic Law and replies, "You know the Law, how do you interpret it?"

The man replied, "Love the LORD your God with all your heart, with all your soul, with all your strength, and with all your mind. And love your neighbor as yourself." Sounds familiar right? As an expert in the Law he was quite familiar with Deuteronomy 6:5 and Leviticus 19:18.

Jesus answered him, "You are correct. Do this and you will live."

Luke writes that the man wanted to justify his actions so he asked a qualifying question, "But, who is my neighbor?" Isn't that interesting? The gospel writer gives us insight into the man's motives. He wanted to justify his prejudice, hatred, and bigotry. He is asking Jesus to define who exactly, and by process of elimination who exactly is not, his "neighbor." Who exactly do I need to love? He's playing the semantics game. This is classic legalism by the way. Legalism is focused on the letter of the law not the heart of the law. This either leaves people extremely rigid or extremely good at finding loopholes around the rules.

If you think I am manipulating the Scripture by pointing out his prejudice, hatred, and bigotry to fit the current topics of our day you need only to pay attention to how Jesus answered.

[79] Luke 10:25-37

To answer the question Jesus tells a parable—he tells a story that illustrates a spiritual truth. You have possibly heard it countless times, but I want to summarize it briefly:

A man was traveling from Jerusalem to Jericho. While on his way he was mugged by a couple of thieves. He was beaten, stripped of his clothes, and left for dead. A priest and a Levite happened to walk along the same way. Upon seeing the man, they bypassed the man and kept walking.

Now, some might be inclined to be hard on the priest and the Levite. Some might even presume to believe they would never do such a heartless thing. But, for both the priest and the Levite, they may have believed the man was already dead. For either of them to touch the man in his condition, especially if he were already dead, would potentially render them ceremonially unclean. If they were headed towards Jerusalem they were likely on their way to perform their ritual duties in the Temple. The sacredness of facilitating the worship of Yahweh was certainly of a higher priority than risking ceremonial uncleanliness to help a man who was possibly already dead. Right?

A Samaritan happened to also walk along the same route. Now, what you need to know about Samaritans is that they were considered half-breeds. There was a tremendous amount of racial, political, and religious tension between the Samaritans and Jews. Centuries before, the Assyrian Empire conquered Israel and deported a number of Israelites. Assyria repopulated the region with other exiled people groups. The remaining Israelites intermarried with the refugees and synchronized their worship practices with that of the foreigner's pagan practices. By Jesus' day, there was tremendous animosity between Jews and Samaritans because the Samaritans were viewed as the byproducts of mixed marriages and mixed religious practices.

The Samaritan saw the man and was moved to compassion. His compassion moved him to act. The Samaritan dressed his wounds with his own oil and wine, bandaged the wounds with strips of his own garments, put the man on his own donkey, took him to a nearby inn, cared for him there, gave the innkeeper two of his own silver coins, and promised to pay the innkeeper whatever other expenses were necessary upon his return. Think about the extravagance of this man's actions towards this wounded Jew. His expression of care and love cost him. His plans were disrupted, his resources were dispensed, and his own prejudices deferred.

Jesus then asked the crowd, "Which of these three do you think was a neighbor to the man who fell into the hands of robbers?"

The expert in the law replied, "The one who had mercy on him."

Jesus told him, "Go and do likewise."

Notice that Jesus answers the man's question not by defining who our neighbors are, but by defining what it looks like for us to be a neighbor. He flips the weight of responsibility from other people to us. Loving our neighbor isn't about the qualifications of other people. Loving our neighbor is about our heart towards people. And not just some people. As it turns out, Jesus calls us to love all people. Even if they are our political, ethnic, and religious enemies.

Jesus' audience would have been a crowd of Jews. Imagine their shock and revulsion at the idea of a Samaritan being the hero of the story. For us, a modern day equivalent might be a Muslim or an illegal immigrant or someone who votes differently than we do. Imagine Jesus coming as a special guest speaker at your church and telling you a story in which an illegal immigrant is an example of what it means to love your neighbor.

Regardless of our political position on an issue, our disposition towards people has to be defined by love. Or else we are missing something that is very dear to the heart of Jesus. By using a Samaritan as an example, Jesus is not justifying the Samaritan's own tendency towards racial hatred either. They were likely just as hateful towards the Jews as the Jews were towards them. Jesus also isn't validating the bad theology of the Samaritans. However, he isn't allowing all his defenses and arguments *against* those people to determine whether they are worthy of love and compassion.

The call of Jesus is clear: Love your fellow human being. This includes your enemies. Gregory Boyd challenges believers to "remain awake to the truth that each person [we] encounter has unsurpassable worth, not because of anything worthwhile [we] happen to see in them, but because their Creator thought them worth dying for."[80] Think about that. God so loved the

---

[80] Gregory A. Boyd, *Present Perfect: Finding God in the Now* (Grand Rapids: Zondervan, 2010), 111.

world that he sent Jesus. God believed everyone was worth his blood. This is where the gospel reaches all the way back to Genesis 1 and recaptures the theological truth that God created humanity in his image. We believe all human life matters. Every person matters. Every person is someone God loves and someone God has called us to love.

So many people get hung up on doctrinal correctness and moral purity. I've met some people who don't drink, smoke, gamble, or have sex with people who are not their spouse. They are morally pure and they have a "biblical" answer for every Sunday school question you could ask. But, they are mean. They don't love people. Dallas Willard writes in his book *The Divine Conspiracy,*

> ...we must realize that deep in our orientations of our spirit we cannot have one posture toward God and a different one toward other people. We are a whole being, and our true character pervades everything we do.[81]

Paul says if we don't love people, rather than making beautiful music, our lives are instead an annoying noise to God and the world.[82]

The Apostle John essentially said the same thing. He essentially suggests that if we do not love people, then we do not

---

[81] Dallas Willard, *The Divine Conspiracy.* (New York: HarperCollins, 1998), 232.

[82] 1 Corinthians 13:1

really have intimate knowledge of God's love. If we do not have intimate knowledge of God's love, then we do not really *know God.*[83]

Love God. Love People.

Compassion

Jesus doesn't give us the liberty to put parameters on who we should love. He also doesn't let us off the hook by just saying in a trivial and superficial way, "Well, yeah, I love people."

Embedded within the parable is the reality that the love Jesus calls us to have is accompanied by action that is compelled by compassion. Verse 33 of Luke 10 says that the Samaritan saw the man and felt compassion for him. Some translations say that he had pity on him. The English translations are trying to capture the meaning of the Greek word *splanchnizomai.* The man felt *splanchnizomai.*

Literally, the word means: "to be moved as to one's bowels, hence to be moved with compassion; to have compassion (for the bowels were thought to be the seat of love and pity)."[84] I thought about titling this chapter, "Bowel Movements," but I figured that might be a little too gross for some. But, really, the word attempts to contain within its meaning the description of that emotion we experience for others that wrenches our

---

[83] 1 John 4

[84] "G4697–splagchnizomai–Strong's Greek Lexicon (kjv)." Blue Letter Bible. Accessed 9 Sep, 2022. https://www.blueletterbible.org/lexicon/g4697/kjv/tr/0-1/.

gut. It attempts to give meaning to the correlation between the physiological and the emotional.

It is not a super common word in the New Testament—it is never used outside of the Synoptic Gospels and is only used in 12 verses. Eight of the twelve verses, Jesus is the subject. He is the one who is moved with compassion. He is the one who sees the crowds of people and his gut is wrenched as he is overwhelmed with love for them because they are like sheep without a shepherd.[85] He is the one who is described as being filled with compassion for a widowed woman who has lost her son.[86] He is the one who is filled with compassion when a blind man asks for the restoration of his sight.[87] He is the one who is moved to compassion when he meets a man with leprosy.[88]

Jesus is moved with compassion and time and time again he acts. He teaches the lost about the good Father. He feeds the hungry, he raises the dead, he opens blind eyes, he heals the sick, and he touches the leper to bring healing. Some of those actions were extremely offensive acts by the way. Touching the unclean leper or healing on the Sabbath or associating with sinners were big "no-no's."

Three of the twelve times the word is used, Jesus uses this word in a parable. One of those three is in this parable about the Good Samaritan. Another use is in the parable of the "Prodigal Son"—when the son is returning home, the Father in

---

[85] Matthew 9:36

[86] Luke 7:13

[87] Matthew 20:34

[88] Mark 1:41

the story sees him a long way off and is filled with compassion.[89] His response? He runs to embrace his son. Which was also socially unacceptable for a dignified man in that culture to do.

The third parable is the one about a Master who is filled with compassion for a servant who owes him a huge debt. His compassion compels him to cancel the servant's debt.[90] But, that servant, in turn, tracks down a man who owed him a smaller debt. He grabs that man around the throat and demands that he pay up. When the Master gets word, he throws the servant in prison. The moral of the story in this parable is that wickedness here is defined as him not showing the same grace, love, and compassion that he was shown.

Through his life and teachings, Jesus consistently reveals something fundamental about God's heart: his heart is moved to compassion. The prodigal son and the debtor reveal that God's heart is not to exact justice and pour out wrath on sinners. Yes, he is just and sin grieves his heart. Injustice rouses his righteous anger. But, like the Master and the Father in the two parables, God's heart is as quickly if not more so moved by compassion.

When God incarnate—when Jesus—encounters suffering, oppression, injustice, disease, and death, his heart is so moved to compassion that his body has a physiological reaction. His stomach sinks and feels heavy. His stomach turns as the chemical response of his compassionate and loving emotions interacts with his physical body—*splanchnizomai.*

---

[89] Luke 15:20

[90] Matthew 18:27

Jesus is the exact representation of the Father (Heb. 1:3). Think about that. How Jesus responds is an exact reflection and representation of God's heart. How Jesus responds to broken, sinful and hurt people is how God responds. What is more profound is that he calls us to go and do likewise.

Do Likewise

One of the biggest things that keeps us from being moved to compassion is our own presuppositions and judgments about other people. Just a brief scroll through any social media feed or comment thread will reveal that people, in general, are really quick to assume the motives of other people. We're really quick to believe we have the clearest perspective on an issue, regardless of our experience, so we offer trite and dismissive solutions to massive problems like public education, gun control, immigration, the refugee crisis, racial injustice, and poverty.

In college, I had a group of friends that really loved sports. I like playing sports, but I am not a big fan of sitting in front of the TV for hours watching games and sportscast episodes on ESPN. I have observed that a large majority of sports fans simply missed their calling. Most sports fans should actually be college football coaches or NBA coaches. The fans always seem to have the clarity to call out the coach's mistake. In fact, if they were calling the shots the team would be undefeated!

I am obviously being a little obnoxious, but my point is that we have a tendency to presume to know our perspectives and opinions on any given issue are right. Whether it is how a sports team should be run or a church, we have our opinions and we are often very quick to voice them. We are about as quick to voice our opinions as we are slow to listen. This tendency will choke out compassion before it even gets a chance.

In the parable, the Samaritan actually had to stop and notice the man on the side of the road. He actually had to slow down enough to take into consideration his situation. Sometimes, like in the parable, for compassion to be worked out we actually have to literally physically stop, slow down, and consider the situation of the other. Other times, stopping and slowing down to consider the other means listening. It means hearing the other's story and allowing their story to intersect with ours. It means not assuming and presuming to know how to help them.

Sometimes our efforts to "fix" problems are about as helpful as one of the characters in the parable saying to the man, "Well, you know you could have avoided this if you didn't travel alone or if you were armed and prepared." While that advice is not necessarily wrong, it is not helpful. The Samaritan didn't assess whether the man's predicament was because of his own error. He didn't stop to consider whether the other person deserved his help based on some sort of biased criteria. No, he stopped and helped the man even though it cost him.

I am extremely passionate about this because I am frequently grieved by the posts I see on social media. I see memes, quotes, and rhetoric shared by self-proclaimed Christians that is... mean. Kindness seems to have been sacrificed on the altar of being "right." People are quick to dismiss any view that doesn't resonate with their own. Rarely, does it seem, people actually stop and ask themselves, "Could I be wrong?"

In the parable, compassion transcended whatever racial differences Jews and Samaritans had against one another. The basic humanity of the other person was more unifying than their differences. If the Samaritan would have denied helping the Jewish man on the side of the road because of their harsh disagreements the man would have likely died. Think about that. I know it's a story, but the implications of our hearts being hardened by our differences is that life and death is on the line.

In *Braving the Wilderness*, Brené Brown writes about the ways we reduce people to issues about which we have an opinion. She describes how the process of dehumanization begins by drawing the "us versus them" line. It feeds off of focusing on the differences so that it feels we do not have anything in common with the other. She writes,

> When we engage in dehumanizing rhetoric or promote dehumanizing images, we diminish our own humanity in the process. When we reduce Muslim people to terrorists or Mexicans to "illegals" or police officers to pigs, it says nothing at all about the people we're attacking. It does, however, say volumes about who we are and the degree to which we're operating in our integrity.[91]

---

[91] Brené Brown, *Braving the Wilderness* (New York: Random House 2017), 75-76.

If we claim to follow Jesus, there is absolutely no room for attitudes that dehumanize other people to exist in our hearts. It not only compromises our integrity, but it misrepresents the Church and thereby misrepresents Jesus. Compassion stands in defiance to our predisposed tendencies to judge, vilify, and hate those people we disagree with.

Maybe we could be slower to speak and quicker to listen. Maybe the ideas we share in conversation or online could be a little more compassionate. Maybe we could start trying to see people through the lens of our common humanity rather than through the lens of our polarizing differences.

Listening is the first step because listening creates the space for compassion to stir. But compassion often prompts action. The action that follows from genuine listening will be prompted by compassion and not by obligation. When we identify with the humanity of other people and we truly believe they are created in the image of God, our hearts will be stirred by their trials, suffering, and injustice.

Sometimes action looks like fostering children. Sometimes it looks like denying ourselves certain luxuries so that we can give of our resources to organizations that help provide clean water to people who need it. Sometimes it looks like researching and understanding the political issues and systems that restrict the opportunities of others and then voting to enact change. Sometimes it looks like not participating in conversations or sharing posts that degrade the dignity of other people. Sometimes it looks like treating the waitress who screwed up your order with dignity. Sometimes it looks like literally loving your neighbor across the street and investing in a relationship with them.

I am not sure what it looks like for you, but if we are going to take Jesus seriously then we need to contextualize what it means to go and do likewise. Doing likewise means dropping our assumptions and judgments. It means putting aside our differences. It means slowing down enough and caring enough to understand the situation of the other so that the appropriate action can follow. We need more people having compassion triggered bowel movements in this world.

Reflection/Discussion Questions

1. What hits your soft spot? What issues or causes or problems in the world awaken your compassion?

2. Who are the Samaritans in your life? Or, to put it another way, who are the people that you find it hard to love?

3. What does it reveal about God's heart that Scripture tells us that Jesus was moved by compassion on so many occasions?

4. What do you think moves his heart to compassion still today? Who are the people and what are the issues that might move Jesus to act if he were physically present on earth right now?

5. What might it look like for you to "go and do likewise"? In what ways can you open your heart up to the same compassion that moved Jesus to act?

CHAPTER 10

Making It Up As We Go

In December 2015, a couple of days before Christmas, my wife mentioned the idea of opening a few gifts from each other early. Even as an adult, I still get a little giddy about opening presents before Christmas Day. My memory of what I got her and my memory of the other gifts she got me has been eclipsed by the one gift I opened that December evening. Emily handed me a baby blue gift bag and sat across from me intently watching as I opened it. I pulled the tissue paper out of the bag to find a pregnancy test, a couple of onesies, and a coffee mug that stated "#1 Dad."

We had been trying, so it wasn't a complete shock. I was excited. At the same time, I didn't really know how I should feel. I've talked to a lot of other dads who have agreed that the emotional experience of the dad is different from that of the mom. For the mom, the little life is growing inside them and is literally a part of them. I experienced an excited expectancy, but also a lot of uncertainty. I had no idea, absolutely no frame of reference, for how drastically this little life was going to change my life.

When Titus was born, all the emotions that were once very abstract and surreal came flooding into my being. I experienced joy and love and….terror. The overwhelmingly beautiful mystery of life comes with a sense of responsibility. Here was a little person. A human being and he was on loan to us from God. He's not mine. I have absolutely no control over his life. I have control over the influence I have in his life, but his life (like all of our lives) is ultimately in God's hands.

We now have two kids, Evelyn was born in 2019. For whatever reason, God has chosen to bestow the magnificent responsibility of stewarding and parenting two little lives to us. It is beautiful, and… It is scary. There are so many things that a non-parent doesn't know about parenting. I "Google" things countless times a week. Which, for the record, I don't recommend doing. There are so many opinions and perspectives on so many things on the internet, that it can be quite discouraging sometimes. Anyhow, the point is that parenting introduces loads of completely new experiences for first-time parents.

A couple of years ago, my sister asked me a question about something related to parenting. In a jokingly-serious sort of way, I said, "We're making this up as we go." That's not totally accurate, but it is somewhat true. On one hand, we are intentional about the love we show, the discipline we practice, and the faith we model. We are informed about the basic, everyday stuff of raising children, and we are doing the best we can to do the best we can. On the other hand, each of our now two kids is different and each stage is different. So there is this reality that we are quite literally learning on the job as we parent.

Spiritual growth is something I believe happens on the job too. When we surrender to Jesus as Lord, we enter into something that Scripture equates to being "born again" and describes as being a "new life." Each stage is different and each person is different. You likely have a different personality than mine, and you certainly have had a different upbringing and a different family of origin. Your story is different, therefore the story of your transformation is going to be different.

However, like parenting, there are a couple of principles and standard practices that can be applied. The need to show love to your kids is a principle, but it may look a little different for each family. Discipline is a principle even though the method may vary. Providing for the needs of your children is a pretty basic thing, but the particular needs may look different. The stages of development happen at a different pace but there are some predictable characteristics.

Likewise, there are spiritual principles that we have talked about in this book. We have talked about the principle of love. Jesus calls us to love God and love others. Our love is to reflect his self-giving, cross-shaped love. Our love is to know no boundaries of race, hate, or state. As our love is transformed to reflect more and more the love of God, we are both compelled and empowered to offer forgiveness, extend grace, and embody compassion.

I sincerely believe that these dispositions of the heart are markers of authentic Christian transformation. I believe those who are intentionally and sincerely following Jesus and who have invited the Spirit of God to change them, will be recognized by the radical nature of their love, forgiveness, grace, and compassion. Jesus said as much, "By this everyone will know that you are my disciples, if you love one another."[92]

If we are being transformed by the Spirit of God it will disrupt our inner life as much as it will clean up our behavior. I don't care if someone doesn't smoke, drink, gamble, watch rated R movies, or have sex with people who are not their spouse. If they do not have love for neighbor, they have missed the heartbeat of God.

I believe this is true, like a principle that is true and transcends time and place. I believe this is as true for the believer in China who is called to forgive their persecutors as it is for the believer in the Bible-belt of America who is called to love their liberal enemies.

However, while I believe these principles are true for all believers, I believe they will look different for each of us as we live them out. For some of us, our first calling is to love and forgive family members who have hurt us deeply. Our participation in the reconciling work of the Kingdom begins with our family. For others of us, God is calling us to partner with a nonprofit organization that works to fight against sex-trafficking. I do not want to prescribe what it will look like for you. What I am challenging you to do is this: begin tilling up the soil of your heart so that it is ready to cultivate the seeds of love, forgiveness, grace, and compassion.

---

[92] John 13:35

Here's Some Ideas

I do not want to prescribe what you should do. So much harm can come from us carrying burdens of "should" that God hasn't placed on our hearts. Yet, for some of you, you would love to have some suggestions. You would like some ideas of where to start. God has exposed something in your heart that he wants to change. He has already begun working to change your mind. For those of you that would like a couple ideas for what it might look like moving forward, here are a few ideas:

Repent

Repentance often has such a connotation of shame. For me, repentance feels like a humiliating act because I feel like repenting of something means I have not only been a *little* wrong, but maybe I have been *grossly* wrong. For example, I have wrestled with going to the "altar" in a worship service when an invitation is given. I have worried in the past about what other people would think. Nobody's perfect, so I am not worried that they may realize that. I fear the narratives that they will make up in their mind about what I am repenting of. Maybe they will think I am repenting of some really bad sin. Repentance, for some reason, seems to be associated with "really bad" sins.

Maybe I sound ridiculous, or maybe you resonate with the inner dialogue that goes through my mind. I just want to point out that the issue is pride. I can't control what other people think. Frankly, it doesn't matter what they think. Repentance is humiliating in that it invites us to humble ourselves before

God. Humility is a great place to start. Humbly acknowledging that we do not have it all figured out invites the One who does have it all figured out to work.

Repentance is more than confession too. Repentance involves a change of direction. Confession simply means stating what is true. We confess that our actions are sinful and wrong in God's eyes. This, on some level, requires a change of mind. Our change of mind inspires a change of direction. For example, confessing of our judgmental spirit simply means we acknowledge and identify that our attitude is wrong. When we repent of our judgmental spirit, it means that the attitude and the behaviors that flowed from that attitude will change too.

Let's say you have a co-worker that you used to think was a horrible sinner because they get super drunk on the weekends, repentance means you will start to see them as a person created in the image of God whom he is longing to extend his grace too. Your conviction of his love for them will begin to impact how you talk to them. Maybe you were short, snarky and dare I say even rude to them before. Perhaps, you were justified in your rudeness too. Maybe they were hostile towards you as a Christian. Repentance will mean that something has changed. Your justifications have been exposed as sinful. Now, your responses and interactions with that person are salted with love and grace.

Repentance always begets action. Not because we have a works-based faith. Repentance begets action because every action begins with a mindset. When our mindset changes our actions follow. Repenting of our selfishness, unforgiveness, harsh legalism, or judgmentalism is a great place to start. And, until we are glorified on the other side, we will never outgrow the need to humbly submit our mindsets to Christ through the act of repentance.

Pray

There are so many great books on prayer. There are so many ways to pray. I believe prayer is as much about sitting in God's presence in silence listening as it is talking to him. What I am going to suggest here is not meant to be an all-encompassing prescription for how to pray. All I can say is that it is really hard to pray for people and hate them at the same time.

The author of Hebrews says that we can come to the throne with boldness, Jesus calls us to pray for our enemies, and Paul says that we should intercede for all people.[93] I believe our prayers make a difference. I believe our prayers are one of the ways that we participate with God in reconciling the world to himself. I believe our prayers participate in the spiritual act of defying the powers of darkness. I believe prayer can influence and impact outcomes.

Beyond all of the ways that I believe prayer can be powerful and effective, I also believe prayer changes us. Richard Foster suggests that prayer's primary purpose is to align our hearts with God's heart. He writes, "The primary purpose of

---

[93] Hebrews 4:16, Matthew 5:44, and 1 Timothy 2:1

prayer is to bring us into [a] life of communion conformed to the image of the Son."[94]

Pray for your enemies, pray for persecuted Christians, pray for refugees, pray for our President, pray for your neighbors, coworkers, and unbelieving friends. As you pray for people, your heart towards people will be shaped by those prayers. It doesn't have to be wordy, eloquent and super-spiritual sounding. Sometimes I literally just say something like, "God, be with (insert name of the person, family, or group)." My prayers are sometimes that short and that simple.

Listen

Listening is such a powerful act. Listening bestows dignity on another person. Everybody wants to be heard and everyone wants to feel understood. As Christ-followers, we should be the best listeners in the world to other people's stories. We should listen to other people's stories because we believe every story matters and every story can be redeemed by Jesus.

We should be slow to speak and quick to listen.[95] Not only do other people's stories matter because they matter to God, but listening to people's stories can help us grow in our understanding. As I have already written about, our compassion and grace for other people is often lacking because we have failed to sympathize with their situation. When we listen to others, we open the door for our hearts to be impacted by their story.

---

[94] Richard Foster, *Prayer: Finding the Heart's True Home* (New York: HarperCollins, 1992) 57.

[95] James 1:19

Back in 2013 while I was a youth pastor, we took a group of students to Nashville, TN for an inner-city mission trip. We partnered with a local church that was located in a rough part of the city. To keep in touch with parents and our congregation, I wrote daily Facebook notes about our activities. Here is an excerpt from Day 6, written on July 28, 2013:

The most impactful thing for me during the day was the opportunity I had to speak with a mother of three of the kids. I walked into the sanctuary to grab something and was almost startled by a woman who was in there with her youngest son holding him as he slept in her arms. I started small talk with her about church; I think I asked if she went to First Wesleyan (our contact church). She said she went to another church, but what she said next convicted my heart. "I go and listen to the sermons but I leave right after cuz' people are so darn judgmental. They think they're all better than me cuz' I have three kids out of wedlock."

She continued to express to me that she knows that having children outside of marriage is not God's will, but she did not know any better. Her father left when she was 15 months old, and it is just a way of life for the women in the projects. She expressed several times that she thinks marriage is a beautiful thing and desires to wait for the right person. She said a lot of women in the projects see marrying a man as a way of escape or for some, having more kids is a way to get more money from the government.

She loves her kids—you can tell just by watching her interact with them. She wants so badly for her kids to grow up and break the generational sin of divorce and broken families. She wants them to rise above the drugs, gangs, shootings, and brokenness they see in the projects where they live. She shared how she believes the Spirit has prompted her to not go home or leave the house when there have been shootings. She believes God protected them. I can say so much about this lady because I was so impressed by her sincere heart and so convicted by my judgmental heart. Pray for her. Her name is Tamica and she wants to raise her kids to be future husbands and future wives who love the Lord.

I had the opportunity and privilege to pray for her and learn from her that sometimes the "poor in spirit" are much closer to the kingdom of God and the heart of God than the churchgoer who considers himself rich in spirit.

Listening to others has changed my life because listening to others has changed my heart towards them. Listening is a great place to begin.

Cultivate Awareness

So many of the issues that have stirred my heart to compassion I would not have known about had someone not informed me. I grew up fairly insulated from so much of the brokenness that affects people on a global scale. I want to share some disturbing statistics with you. I want to warn you first. I was exposed to some of these issues during my time at a Christian university, often during a chapel service. Sometimes I walked away so overwhelmed and discouraged. I felt so utterly helpless to make even a dent in the issues that are so many people's reality.

I am not sharing these statistics with you to discourage you. I am not sharing these statistics to guilt you into giving thousands of dollars to an organization. I am not sharing these issues with you so that you do anything about these particular issues at all. I am sharing them because awareness is a starting point. On your own, you can't make a dent in any of these issues, but together we can.

Maybe one of these issues will stir your heart to act. Maybe you will volunteer, give, or advocate. Maybe you will change your spending habits or eating habits. Maybe not. Maybe you will continue to invest your time and energy in other issues. Maybe your awareness of these issues will simply help you pray more specifically.

My family has a policy we abide by. We have chosen the causes that we are going to say "yes" to. We have chosen where we are giving our money. Anything outside of those things we have already said "yes" to are a guilt-free "we will pray about it, but for now it is a 'no'" answer. Sometimes we have prayed about something and God prompted us to give a specific amount for that specific issue. Other times, we have prayed about something and felt a peace about saying "no."

Please do not walk away from this portion of the chapter with a guilt-induced desire to be charitable. Rather, realize that there is plenty of opportunities to be salt and light in our world. At the very least, resolve in your heart that you will be salt and light in whatever way God is calling you.

I would also ask that you allow your awareness of these issues to soften your heart towards the poor, the refugee, the foreigner, and the marginalized of the world. So many people have an "America First" mindset. Listen, I love America, but I believe I have been invited to participate with Jesus in his global mission. I believe Jesus loves the world and has called me to cultivate a love for the world in my own heart. Below are some global issues that have stirred my heart.

Global poverty statistics as cited on Compassion International's website:[96]

- More than 736 million people worldwide live below the poverty line — measured by the World Bank as earning less than $1.90 per day.
- Child poverty accounts for half of the world's poor with 1 out of 5 children experiencing extreme poverty.
- One out of every 27 children will die before reaching the age of 5, mostly from malnutrition and other preventable causes due to extreme poverty.
- Poverty rose globally in 2020 and 2021 by 150 million people — the first increase in the global poverty rate in 20 years.
- More than 785 million people globally do not have access to basic water services, including a well.

---

[96] "Poverty Facts and Statistics to Better Understand Global Poverty," Compassion International, accessed September 9, 2022, https://www.compassion.com/poverty/poverty.htm

- One-fourth of the world's total population (roughly 2 billion people) do not have basic sanitation like a toilet in their home.
- The global COVID-19 pandemic is expected to set back poverty reduction progress in 70 developing countries by three to 10 years.

Clean water is an issue for a large part of the world. The World Health Organization shares these facts on their website:[97]

- Globally, at least 2 billion people use a drinking water source contaminated with faeces.
- Over 2 billion people live in water-stressed countries, which is expected to be exacerbated in some regions as result of climate change and population growth.
- Microbiologically contaminated drinking water can transmit diseases such as diarrhoea, cholera, dysentery, typhoid and polio and is estimated to cause 485,000 diarrhoeal deaths each year.

---

[97] "Drinking Water," World Health Organization, accessed September 9, 2022, https://www.who.int/news-room/fact-sheets/detail/drinking-water#:~:text=In%202020%2C%2074%25%20of%20the,needed%2C%20and%20free%20from%20contamination.

Human Trafficking is another major global issue. Here are some disturbing facts:[98]

- It's estimated that internationally there are between 20 million and 40 million people in modern slavery today. Assessing the full scope of human trafficking is difficult because many cases so often go undetected, something the United Nations refers to as "the hidden figure of crime."
- Human trafficking earns global profits of roughly $150 billion a year for traffickers, $99 billion of which comes from commercial sexual exploitation.
- In 2018, over half (51.6%) of the criminal human trafficking cases active in the US were sex trafficking cases involving only children.
- Reports indicate that a large number of child sex trafficking survivors in the US were at one time in the foster care system.

God has called us to participate with him in his global mission of reconciling the world to himself through Jesus Christ. Part of being light in the darkness is combatting all forms of darkness in our world. Part of participating in God's global mission is cultivating a heart that cares about global issues. This starts with awareness.

---

[98] "11 Facts about Human Trafficking," DoSomething.org, accessed September 9, 2022, https://www.dosomething.org/us/facts/11-facts-about-human-trafficking.

Invest Your Resources

For some of us, there will be some very specific causes that will burden our hearts. Compassion compels action remember? Part of being Good News people is that we live it out. We are salt and light. We shine in dark places and bring hope to hopeless circumstances. We proclaim the Good News in word and deed. We certainly do this by proclaiming the truth that Jesus has reconciled us to God through his death and resurrection so that we can be made right with him. Sometimes we also do this in very tangible ways.

Giving financially to Kingdom causes is not just a sacrifice. It is an investment. We may never reap the rewards of our investment in this life, but when we give to things that make an eternal difference we will reap an eternal reward. Investing in Kingdom work cultivates hope and works towards seeing God's will enacted on earth as in heaven. I don't mean to frame giving as an "investment" in a manipulative way. Giving of our resources or even giving of our time does require some level of sacrifice. It's just that in the Kingdom economy it is more blessed to give than receive and sacrifice gives way to resurrection hope.

Acts of Defiance

For some of us, God is calling us to put these biblical concepts into practice. We can't just talk about the ideas in this book over coffee with our small group. We have to do something. We have to act.

Some of us need to forgive. Forgiveness feels costly because the other person may not deserve forgiveness. This might look like you praying for the person who has hurt you. As you pray for God's best for them, God will heal your heart. It may mean that you need to make a phone call and set up a time to meet in person with someone. You may have to ask God to help you forgive each and every day for a long time. I don't know the specifics, but some of you need to resolve to forgive.

Others of you need to interact with your neighbors or coworkers. Instead of viewing them with indifference, God is calling you to embody the gospel of grace to them. This might start by you engaging in conversations, inviting them to lunch, or inviting them over to your house for dinner. God might be calling you to engage with the people in your sphere of influence who do not yet know him.

For some of you, God is stirring you to take a more activist approach. Maybe you are burdened by the realities of global poverty. Several great, faith-based organizations have child-sponsorship programs. For a little more than 2 coffee snob latte's a week, you can sponsor a child and open up a whole new world of possibilities for their future.

Maybe you have been blessed financially and you want to financially partner with organizations that work to provide clean water for people living in underdeveloped regions. Maybe you can partner with an organization that is working to fight against human trafficking. Again, there are a number of great faith-based organizations that do this sort of work.

Maybe you are really in touch with how policies and structures contribute to systemic issues of poverty in our country. Maybe God has positioned you and called you to advocate for the marginalized of our nation's people by how you vote. Maybe instead of regurgitating partisan rhetoric and propaganda, you will direct that energy towards promoting a cause that serves the least of these. Maybe, like me, you will be careful about how you talk about racial reconciliation, immigration, and refugees. Your politics may not change, but maybe your perspective has shifted from only seeing issues to seeing the people affected by the issues.

Maybe you will volunteer for a pregnancy care center in your local town. Your heart for the unborn has always been steadfast, but maybe God is calling you to mentor young moms instead of judging them. Maybe you could volunteer at your local homeless shelter. Maybe you will volunteer by giving your time to a prison ministry.

I know some people have been so moved by the Good News of Jesus that they have adopted children out of the foster care system. I know sometimes people view adoption as an option for couple's who cannot have children, but I know of couples who have biological children and have also chosen to adopt. They chose to adopt because they wanted to change the trajectory of a child's life in Jesus' name.

Maybe God is stirring you to literally sell your possessions and move to another country as a foreign missionary. Instead of viewing Muslims as the enemies of America, your heart has been moved to see them as people whom God loves. Perhaps you feel called to minister to Muslim refugees in Europe.

I don't know what it will look like for you, but I want to encourage you to follow through with the stirrings in your heart. Take the first step. Research organizations that do the sort of work that your heart is burdened to do. Don't allow your compassion to dry up. Find some way to live it out. Whether it is inviting your coworker to lunch or looking into adoption, do something. Find ways to be a blessing, be generous, be gracious, be a good news person in Jesus' name.

Every act of love, grace, forgiveness, and compassion is an act of defiance. These acts defy the kingdom of darkness by suffocating the evil that empowers it. Love, grace, forgiveness, and compassion are the way of victory because they are the way of Jesus. Follow Jesus. Defy darkness. Join the revolution.

Reflection/Discussion Questions

1. Being a Christian is about more than just going to heaven when we die. Being a Christian is about following Jesus, and that is a journey involving new and different stages. How has following Jesus shaped and changed how you live?

2. Are there any mindsets, attitudes, or heart postures that you have been convicted to repent of?

3. Are there any people or causes that God is prompting you to add to your prayer list?

4. What might it look like for you to be quicker to listen and slower to speak?

5. Are there any ways God's Spirit is prompting you to raise awareness or generously invest your resources?

6. How are you going to participate in acts that defy darkness?

Acknowledgements

Emily,
Thank you for being my best friend, my partner in life, and a constant source of encouragement. Thank you for supporting this project and for believing in me.

Titus and Evelyn,
Thank you for the privilege of being your dad. (And for providing numerous real-life illustrations).

Mom,
Thank you for teaching me at a young age to be hospitable, friendly, and kind to people.

Dad,
Thank you for always reminding me that you were proud of me and for constantly asking, "Son, when are you going to write that book." I wish you would have been able to hold the finished product.

Victoria,
Thank you for listening to me as I navigated the publishing journey, and encouraging me to go for it.

Chris,
Thank you for setting an example of how to pursue goals with intentionality.

Jenni Cannariato and Double Check Editing,
Thank you for helping me refine my writing.

Kim Small and the team at Xulon Press,
Thank you for walking with me on this publishing journey.

King Jesus,
Thank you for loving me and rescuing me and inviting me to participate in Kingdom work. May the words of these pages glorify you and help others encounter you more fully.

CPSIA information can be obtained
at www.ICGtesting.com
Printed in the USA
BVHW031611090223
658201BV00006B/378